Put Another Plate on the Table

I'm Coming Home

Created By:

Laura J. Behan

Illustrations & Photos:

Contributed by James C. Behan

First Edition

October, 2013

Flushing, Michigan

Michwoman@aol.com

Author's Note

I have always been fascinated with historical events, people & places. Until I wrote this book I didn't know a tremendous amount about World War II. My father told stories about his experiences from time to time and my siblings and I have always known that this was a period in his life that he held close to his heart and memory. I'm one of his six children – four boys and two girls. In birth order, I rank the fifth born.

Now a middle-aged woman with a grown son of my own, I have read Dad's letters and felt compelled to share them. I live a modest life in Michigan as a typical American middle-class citizen. I'm one of the people born in the last years of the "baby-boomer" era. I feel very strongly that our predecessors should not be forgotten, for they are the ones who fought to preserve our dreams.

Dedicated with heart-felt gratitude to anyone who has unselfishly served in the United States Military desiring only to defend our Country and our way of life, as well as those who remained at home waiting and praying for them to return safely.

Setting the Stage

This written journey is primarily authored by the letters that were sent home by my father James Behan (Hereafter referred to as "Dad") while he was in the United States Navy in World War II. He enlisted right out of High School at age 17 in July of 1943 and remained there until he was 20 ½ in April of 1946. He would mature by at least a decade in those 3 ½ short years. When my siblings and I would ask him why he joined so quickly and readily he would answer:

"That's just what you did in those days – that's what everyone did."

A short story about the years he spent growing up in the Mott Park area of Flint, Michigan, will help to explain many of the comments and people to whom these letters are addressed.

He was born in Mishawaka, Indiana, in 1925. Like so many people did during that time his family moved to Flint in the early 20th century so his Father could find work in an exploding automotive industry. Dad is the oldest of three children – one younger sister named Patricia (Patsy) and the youngest child Robert (Bobbie).

Soon after moving to Flint, his Father became an alcoholic who would take his weekly pay directly to the local bar and proceed to get drunk, come home and abuse Dad's Mother both verbally & physically. One day, at about age 15, Dad had enough of this behavior and physically got in between his parents and threatened his Father using a vintage sword letting him know that he could not mistreat his Mother again. At that moment his father backed off. A very short time after that his Mother was found dead while she slept in her bed from an apparent heart attack. Dad always said that his Father drove his Mother to her grave.

Since my grandfather was in no condition to care for the 3 children, all 4 of them moved in with Dad's Aunt Rose (his Mother's sister) who had married a man named Frank Cook. They lived just across from the local park so the move was not far and they all remained close to their familiar environment. Interestingly, Rose & Frank never had children of their own.

Frank Cook was a World War I Bomber Pilot and his nickname was "Cookie" – which is all I ever knew him as. There are letters written just to him in which Dad refers to him as "Bummer" and refers to himself as "The Sissy". We believe these nicknames were created because Dad had joined the Navy instead of the Air Force as Cookie had done.

While living with Rose & Cookie, Dad's Father once almost burned their house down by falling asleep with a lit cigarette. Cookie booted him out and he ended up in some kind of rooming house near the factory where he worked. He eventually passed away from a failed liver while Dad was overseas during the war. Nobody wanted to pay for a funeral for him so he was buried in the City Cemetery until Dad could afford to move him years later to the Cemetery where the other members of the family are resting. Rose & Cookie became the equivalent of parents to Dad, Patsy and Bobbie - and grandparents to me and my siblings and our cousins. Dad never mentions his father's death in any of these letters.

Dad does mention several of the friends he graduated from High School with in these letters. I still have his senior year scrapbook that has the autographs and well wishes of these young men. They all miraculously survived the war and reunited afterward. Ironically, Dad ended up outliving all of them. The name you see the most is Funce Etue – Dad's very close buddy in school. He was also great friends with Bob Donnelly, Bert Hamilton & Jack Chatterson – all of whom are mentioned in these letters.

I've re-typed the letters so they are easily legible. Dad was not the best speller in the world so I corrected most of his errors in my typed versions to make the reading flow better. I found that he used the word "swell" frequently. I suppose it was equivalent to my generation using "cool".

Some of these letters are on what was called "V-mail", short for "Victory Mail" which was used during World War II. It was the primary and secure method to correspond with soldiers stationed abroad. A V-mail letter would be censored, copied to film, and printed back to paper upon arrival at its destination. Equally interesting are the letters that the Navy censors literally cut parts out of with scissors, and one that they removed a photo from. In one of them he mentions that several of his letters were totally rejected by the censors and returned undelivered. The "passed" stamps can be seen on several of them.

I've learned more about World War II than I ever knew before just by reading these letters and doing research to learn about the verbiage used and the items he collected.

Finally – Just a note to explain a couple other things. One – the things you see in red text are my words to help explain what I thought might need clarification. Two - you will see some letters addressed to "Ozie" or "Irish". Dad called his Aunt Rose "Ozie" sometimes. I believe he probably couldn't pronounce the "R" when he was a toddler and the nickname stuck. He called his brother Bobbie "Irish" and I really do not know where that nickname came from.

Reading these letters tell quite the story of what life was like for a very young man in a very tumultuous war while being far from his home.

Every letter, picture & piece of memorabilia in this book was taken from Dad's personal collection. He treasured them and I believe he would be happy to share them.

My hope is that you can see in your mind's eye the story as it was occurring the same way I did.

Bon Voyage!

Terms You Will See And What They Mean

USS Dobbin (AD 3)   "AD" Means this ship is a Destroyer Tender. The "3" means it's the 3rd ship in that series. Only 8 ships in this series were built. A Destroyer Tender's job is to "tend" to a squadron of destroyers. They provided torpedoes, ammunition, food & medical support. They were targeted for attack more often than the destroyers in order to disrupt the supplies getting to their destination.

Ruptured Duck   This was a lapel pin given to military service members who were discharged under honorable conditions during World War II. It was originally created as an Eagle but was given the Ruptured Duck nickname soon after its creation because of its appearance.

Fish   Nickname for torpedoes

TM 2/c   This was Dad's military rank designation when he was discharged – Torpedo Man Second Class.

A.A.   "Anti-Aircraft"

WHERE IT ALL BEGAN

"Yesterday, December 7, 1941 — a date which will live in infamy — the United States was suddenly and deliberately attacked by naval and air forces of the Empire of Japan. Always will we remember the character of the onslaught against us. No matter how long it may take us to overcome this premeditated invasion, the American people, in their righteous might, will win through to absolute victory."

— President Franklin D. Roosevelt
Address To Congress, December 8, 1941

The Japanese also attacked and
subsequently occupied Manila,
Philippines, on December 7, 1941

Dad with his father –
High School Graduation

Proud Graduate

GOOD LUCK JIMMY.

Drawings done in Dad's
High School Senior
Scrapbook

SOLDIER!

Best buddies just out of
High School and before
going off to war

Boot Camp – Great Lakes Naval Training Station, Illinois

GREAT LAKES N.T.S.
CAMP PORTER Co. # 1316   SEPT.-OCT.-NOV. 1943

Dear Rose & all

We arrived here at 1:00 last night. Got to bet about 1:00, hit the deck this morning at 5:30. Please excuse the writing as I am sitting on the edge of my bunk. In about 5 minutes we are going to chow, then I have to stand gaurd from 6:00 to 8:00. We would have to stand 4 hours ordinarily, but we have a pretty good C.O. (Commanding Officer) so we only have to stand 2 hours. We will probably be shipped to another Camp Friday or Saturday. Right now I am in Camp Barry. I hope I get shipped to Green Bay because Stu & Donnelly are there. Don't try to answer this because I haven't received my full address yet.

Love to all

Jim

P.S. Say hello to Daddy for me, and I will write as soon as I get stationed

Dear Rose & All

We arrived here at 12:00 last night. Got to bed about 1:00,
Hit the deck this morning at 5:30. Please excuse the writing as
I am sitting on the edge of my bunk. In about 15 minutes we
are going to chow, then I have to stand guard from 6:00 to 8:00.
We would have to stand 4 hours ordinarily, but we have a
pretty good C.O. (Commanding Officer) so we only have to stand
2 hours. We will probably be shipped to another camp Friday or
Saturday. Right now I am in Camp Barry. I hope to get shipped
to Green Bay because Etue & Donnelly are there. Don't try to
answer this because I haven't received my full address yet.

Love to all,

Jim

P.S. Say Hello to Daddy For me, and I will
write as soon as I get stationed

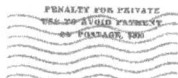

U. S. Naval Training Station
Great Lakes, Ill.   November 12 1943

Name JAMES C. BEHAN   Company No. 1212

Has been transferred and will notify you of his new address. Do not
address any more mail to him at this address.

The Commanding Officer.

NTSGL—5-21-43—12634

Jan 20, 1944

"Dear" Bummer

I received the knife and
the case yesterday. I meant to
write yesterday and thank you for
sending it but I had a date to
jockey a swab around the shop.
The knife is just what I wanted,
its just the right length & everything.
The holster is really slick, everybody
that saw it wanted to know
where I got it because you can't
buy them around here. I really

appreciate you sending it because I
couldn't have bought one as good any
where. I'll be home some time
Sunday night on the bus from
Detroit. I have to take a train
from Norfolk to Toledo and from Toledo
to Detroit. However the trains may
be late as they usually are so if
I don't get in on that bus I'll be
on the next one. I guess I'd
better shove off now I have another
date with a swab, so take care
and thanks again for the swell knife

Sissy !

Jan 20, 1944

"Dear" Bummer,

I received the knife and the case yesterday. I meant to write yesterday and thank you for sending it but I had a date to jockey a swab around the shop.

The knife is just what I wanted, it's just the right length & everything. The holster is really slick, everybody that saw it wanted to know where I got it because you can't buy them around here. I really appreciate you sending it because I couldn't have bought one as good anywhere. I'll be home some time Sunday night on the bus from Detroit. I have to take a train from Norfolk to Toledo and from Toledo to Detroit. However the trains may be late as they usually are so if I don't get in on that bus I'll be on the next one. I guess I'd better shove off now. I have another date with a swab, so take care and thanks again for the swell knife.

Sissy!

Feb 4, 1944

Dear Rose & all

    This is the first chance I've had to write to you. I arrived here about 8:00 PM. Feb 1 and I've been trying to get squared around ever since. The climate is nice here. It rains about twice a day because its the rainy season, but the sun always comes out and dries everything up. The rain just seems to clean the air. I could have gone on liberty last night and tonight but I have been to busy getting settled. From what I've seen of San Diego its a lot cleaner than Norfolk, and the people treat you swell. at least they really treated me swell. This school I'm going to is a practical school lasting 8 weeks. I wont get another promotion out of it because you have to go to sea before your eligible for 2nd class T.M. I'm going to try and contact Bert as soon as I can but it will probably be next week some time.

2

    I really enjoyed the trip coming down here. We came through the Rocky Mountains and did it ever seem funny to see green grass and oranges growing on trees. Well Rose I guess I have to stop now. I'll tell you more next time. Write real soon

        Love to all
        Jim

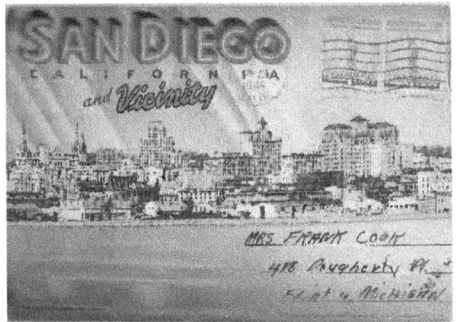

MRS FRANK COOK
418 Dougherty St.
Apt. 4 Michigan

Arrival in San Diego for practical training before going out to sea

Feb 4, 1944

Dear Rose & All,

This is the first chance I've had to write to you. I arrived here about 8:00 PM Feb 2 and I've been trying to get squared around ever since. The climate is nice here. It rains about twice a day because it's the rainy season, but the sun always comes out and dries everything up. The rain just seems to clean the air. I could have gone on liberty last night and tonight but I have been busy getting settled. From what I've seen of San Diego it's a lot cleaner than Norfolk, and the people treat you swell, at least they really treated me swell. This school I'm going to is a practical school lasting 8 weeks. I won't get another promotion out of it because you have to go to sea before you're eligible for 2nd class T.M. I'm going to try and contact Bert as soon as I can but it will probably be next week some time.

I really enjoyed the trip coming down here. We came through the Rocky Mountains and did it ever seem funny to see green grass and oranges growing on trees. Well Rose I guess I'll have to stop now. I'll tell you more next time. Write real soon.

Love to All

Jim

OUR BARRACKS LIKE THIS !

Dear Rose

    These are my diplomas from Torpedo school in Norfolk. The mark of 3.28 was the mark on my Petty Officer test – my final mark was 3.43. Put these in a safe place. I may need them some day.

               Love
               Jim

Torpedo School, Norfolk, Virginia, Nov - Dec 1943 - Jan - 1944   Class 10-44

TOP ROW Left to Right   Middle Row   Bottom Row

Earl Kelly   Philip D. Geo.   Leslie a Drew
W. Finnigan   Richard H. Coon   George L. Long
Gerald B. Dial   Paul J. Fisher   Chief - Billings
Jim Behan   Fred A. Gogo   Donald Mann
H. P. Conrady   George Coffohn
Paul Calhoon   Dale Gordon

Dear Rose

This is the picture of the fellows that
were in my class room. There a couple of
old goats amongst us but most of the guys
are 22 or under. Besides the ones in the picture
there is 44 more fellows in my class
Love
Jim

Dear Rose

    This is the picture of the fellows that were in my class
room. There's a couple of old goats amongst us but most of the
guys are 22 or under. Besides the ones in the picture there is 44
more fellows in my class.

Love,
Jim

March 31, 1944

Dear Rose + all

I received the big box today. Everything is whole & unbroken. They sure are delicious, the cookies & cakes I mean. Especially after eating this chow around here. They really hit the spot. All the guys that I gave a taste to, said to tell you there delicious and that they wished they had an aunt like mine. I like the way you put the chocolate on the tops of the little cakes. You remembered I like them extra thick with frosting. I also enjoyed the paper that you put in the top. You asked me what I wanted for Easter. There is nothing I need. But I would enjoy some cookies & cakes like you sent today.

I was sorry to hear about Joe Dolan. He use to hang around Barber's a lot. All of us knew him. I saw him the last time I was home and he asked me how I was getting along.

We took our final today. It sure was a relief to get that over. It took me 7 hours & 13 minutes to write it. Tommorow we graduate. I'll send you the diploma as soon as I get it. Our Chief invited all the guys in the class up to his house for dinner tonight. He lives here in Diego and he's always bragging about his wifes cooking, so were going to find out for ourselves. He's a swell guy. He's been in the Navy 26 years and never had a report against him. Well Rose I'd better get going. He promised us steaks so I don't want to miss it. Thanks again for the swell cookies and cakes. There much better than any chow I could get here. Love to all

Jim

17

March 31, 1944

Dear Rose & All,

I received the big box today. Everything is whole & unbroken. They sure are delicious, the cookies & cakes I mean, especially after eating the chow around here. They really hit the spot. All the guys that I gave a taste to said to tell you they're delicious and that they wished they had an Aunt like mine. I like the way you put the chocolate on the tops of the little cakes. You remembered I like them extra thick with frosting. I also enjoyed the paper that you put in the top. You asked me what I wanted for Easter. There is nothing I need but I would enjoy some cookies and cakes like you sent today.

I was sorry to hear about Joe Dolan. He use to hang around Barber's a lot. All of us knew him. I saw him the last time I was home and he asked me how I was getting along.

We took our final today. It sure was a relief to get that over. It took me 7 hours & 13 minutes to write it. Tomorrow we graduate. I'll send you the diploma as soon as I get it. Our Chief invited all the guys close up to his house for dinner tonight. He lives here in Diego and he's always bragging about his wife's cooking so we're going to find out for ourselves. He's a swell guy. He's been in the Navy 26 years and never had a report against him.

Well Rose I'd better get going. He promised us steaks so I don't want to miss it. Thanks again for the swell cookies and cakes. They're much better than any chow I could get here.

Love to all,

Jim

March 31, 1944

Dear Rose + all

Today I graduated. Enclosed is my diploma. The Mark 3.45 is the score I made on my T.M. 3/c test. The Mark 3.56 is my final average for this school. There was 60 guys altogether in my class. My mark was 4th highest in the class, ahem! I've been recommended for T.M. 3/c now all I need is time on sea or overseas duty to get it. The perfect score was 4.0. Lucky Finnigan has been assigned to East Coast Command. That means sea duty off the East coast and probably delayed orders to New York or Norfolk

Rose - 1944

where he will pick up a ship. We might be lucky enough to get the Shangra La which is at Philadelphia according to scuttlebutt.

I received a letter from France today so Im enclosing it to.

My address has been changed here it is

Fleet Torpedo School
Aerial Unit 316 Section 4
U.S. Naval Repair Base
San Diego 36, California

Will Rose I guess I'll close now. I'll write again tomorrow

Love to all
Jim

P.S. Tell Patsy I received the letter with the dollar. I'll write her tomorrow.

March 31, 1944

Dear Rose & All,

Today I graduated. Enclosed is my diploma. The mark 3.45 is the score I made on my T.M. 2/c test. The mark 3.56 is my final average for this school. There was 60 guys altogether in my class. My mark was 4th highest in the class, ahem! I've been recommended for T.M. 2/c. Now all I need is time at sea or overseas duty to get it. The perfect score was 4.0. Lucky Finnigan has been assigned to East Coast Command. That means sea duty off the East Coast and probably delayed orders to New York or Norfolk where he will pick up a ship. He might be lucky enough to get the Shangra La which is at Philadelphia according to scuttlebutt.

I received a letter from Funce today so I'm enclosing it too.

My address has been changed – here it is

> Fleet Torpedo School
>
> Aerial Unit 316 Section 4
>
> U.S. Naval Repair Base
>
> San Diego 36, California

Well Rose I guess I'll close now. I'll write again tomorrow.

> Love to all,
>
> Jim

P.S. Tell Patsy I received the letter with the dollar. I'll write her tomorrow.

May 8th, 1944
Monday Nite

Dear Patsy,
I received your air mail letter of the
2nd and your other letter of the third. This
week were on Seamanship and we have an
old Chief who has been in the Navy 22 years.
He sure has a lot of stories about his
experiences all over the world that he
tells us. He tries to talk us into
staying in the navy 20 years. But he's
waisting his breath as far as I'm
concerned. Sorry to hear that a spring
cold has caught up to you, hurry up
and shake it. No Patsy there isn't anything
that I really need, but thanks for
offering anyway. As for the cookies I
dont have to tell you how welcome

they would be.
How many more weeks before
you'll be out of school? I suppose you
have the days counted.
Well Patsy I haven't anything else
to say tonight, so I'll stop. Tell
Rosemary I'll answer her letter as
soon as I can.

Love
Jim

Love
Your
Sister
Patsy
1-77-45

21

May 8th, 1944
Monday Nite

Dear Patsy,

I received your air mail letter of the 2nd and your other letter of the third. This week we're on Seamanship and have an old Chief who has been in the Navy 32 years. He sure has a lot of stories bout his experiences all over the world that he tells us. He tries to talk us into staying in the Navy 20 years. But he's wasting his breath as far as I'm concerned. Sorry to hear that a spring cold has caught up to you, hurry up and shake it. No Patsy there isn't anything that I really need, but thanks for offering anyway. As for the cookies I don't have to tell you how welcome they would be.

How many more weeks before you'll be out of school? I suppose you have the days counted.

Well Patsy I haven't anything else to say tonight so I'll stop. Tell Rosemary I'll answer her letter as soon as I can.

Love to all,

Jim

June 1, 1944

Dear Rose

I sent you a telegram this morning as soon as my name was posted so that you'd know where I am. They say our mail will be censored when we get there, however I don't know if this is true. Rose the Chief told us we might be in Frisco for a couple weeks and then will be assigned to an overseas base or a ship. I've been waiting for this so I'm glad of it. I don't want you or anyone to worry about me because it won't do any good for anyone.

I'll do my best to let you know where I am all the time. So if I say anything you don't understand just try and figure it out and you'll have a pretty good idea where I am. I'm telling you this now because they may censor outgoing mail up there. I know its going to be pretty hard on you now that Cookie has gone north. Bobby will be the man of the house now eh? I'm glad the movie film turned out good. I'd like to see it, but I look like I'm just out of "boots". Rose there is a chance that

---

I might get home too. If I'm assigned to a new ship which is being built. they might let me come home. I hope I do get a chance but I won't be disappointed if I don't. Keep praying & maybe I will?

Maybe some day when its all over we can take a trip. I'd like to show you some of the things I've seen, I know you'd enjoy them.

Rose I may not get a chance to write again before I leave Dago because we'll be awful busy taking, physicals, lashing gear & so

---

on along with the rest of our daily duties. This is about all the news I have today. I'll try and write again before we leave.

Take Care of Yourself &
take it Easy

Love.

Jim

June 1, 1944

Dear Rose

I sent you a telegram this morning as soon as my name was posted so that you'd know where I am. They say our mail will be censored when we get there, however I don't know if this is true. Rose the Chief told us we might be in Frisco for a couple weeks and then we'll be assigned to an overseas base or a ship. I've been waiting for this so I'm glad of it. I don't want you or anyone to worry about me because it won't do any good for anyone.

I'll do my best to let you know where I am all the time. So if I say anything you don't understand just try and figure it out and you'll have a pretty good idea where I am. I'm telling you this now because they may censor outgoing mail up there. I know it's going to be pretty hard on you now that Cookie has gone north. Bobby will be the man of the house now eh? I'm glad the movie film turned out good. I'd like to see it, bet I look like I'm just out of "boots".

Rose there is a chance that I might get home too. If I'm assigned to a new ship which is being built they might let me come home. I hope I do get a chance but I won't be disappointed if I don't. Keep praying and maybe I will?

Maybe someday when it's all over we can take a trip. I'd like to show you some of the things I've seen. I know you'd enjoy them.

Rose I may not get a chance to write again before I leave Diego because we'll be awful busy taking physicals, locking gear & so on along with the rest of our daily duties. This about all the news I have today. I'll try and write again before we leave.

Take Care of Yourself &
Take it easy.
Love,
Jim

UNITED STATES NAVY

June 4, 1944
Sunday Nite

Dear Rose & all,

We just heard over the radio that Rome fell this morning, that's good news. I hope they can keep on going. We leave San Diego tomorrow morning at 8:00 O'clock. I'm all set to go and we have a few minutes till taps so I thought I'd drop you a line. We really have been busy so I didn't have much time to write. Tell Mrs. Etre I'll answer her letter as soon as I can.

I am really tired out so I'll close for now. I'll write again as

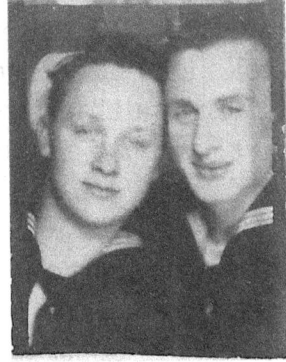

2

soon as I get my new address.
So Long
Love to all
Jim

P.S. I finished the cookies today, they were swell !!!

June 4, 1944
Sunday Nite

Dear Rose & All,

We just heard over the radio that Rome fell this morning, that's good news I hope they can keep on going. We leave San Diego tomorrow morning at 8:00 O'clock. I'm all set to go and have a few minutes till taps so I thought I'd drop you a line.

We really have been busy so I didn't have much time to write. Tell Mrs. Etue I'll answer her letter as soon as I can.

I'm really tired out so I'll close for now. I'll write again as soon as I get my new address.

So Long

Love to all,

Jim

P.S. I finished the
cookies today, they were swell!!!

June 6, 1944
(D Day)

Dear Rose & all

This morning when we had reville on the train they told us the good news. We were on a troop train and you should have heard the noise when they gave us the news. We had a pullman all the way. They really treated us like kings. Whenever we stopped, the red cross or Navy mothers had coffee & donuts for us. This Treasure Island is a very beautiful place. They had the worlds fair here a few years ago and turned the buildings and grounds over to the Navy.

I can see the "Golden Gate" bridge from here also alcatraz island which is out in the middle of the bay.

According to the dope we get today we will be here about for 3 weeks. They send most of them to Pearl Harbor and then ~~assign~~ em to duty from there. Thats all I know.

Rose I wish you would say a special prayer for France Steele He's in on that invasion and is probably going through hell. That was the first thing I thought of when I heard about it, I hope he comes through O.K.

Right now the whole barracks is listening to President Roosevelt. You

could hear a pin drop.

I saw a lot of interesting things today but I'm kind of tired tonight so I'll tell you about them in my next letter. Don't worry about me I'm fine. Say hello to everyone for me.

Love to all
Jim

P.S. I received cookies letters and the $5.00 bill just before I left Diego. Thanks a lot.

To Jim
"Best of Luck"
FUNCE

Sept 14-1944

27

June 6, 1944
(D-Day)

Dear Rose & All,

This morning when we had revile on the train they told us the good news. We were on a troop train and you should have heard the noise when they gave us the news. We had a Pullman all the way. They really treated us like kings. Whenever we stopped, the Red Cross or Navy mothers had coffee & donuts for us. This Treasure Island is a very beautiful place. They had the world's fair here a few years ago and turned the buildings and grounds over to the Navy. I can see the "Golden Gate" bridge from here – also Alcatraz Island which is out in the middle of the bay.

According to the dope we got today we will be here about 2 or 3 weeks. They send most of them to Pearl Harbor and then assign 'em to duty from there. That's all I know.

Rose I wish you would say a special prayer for Funce Etue. He's in on that invasion and is probably going through hell. That was the first thing I thought of when I heard about it. I hope he comes through O.K.

Right now the whole barracks is listening to President Roosevelt. You could hear a pin drop. I saw a lot of interesting things today but I'm kind of tired tonight so I'll tell you about them in my next letter. Don't worry about me I'm fine. Say hello to everyone for me.

Love to all,

Jim

P.S. I received Cookie's letter and the $5.00 bill just before I left Dago. Thanks a lot.

June 11, 1944
Sunday afternoon

Dear Rose & all

Good afternoon Mrs. Cook hows everything with you? I went to Mass in the chapel here on the base this morning. They have creeping bent grass growing around it and a lot of different color flowers growing. I wish you could see it, I thought of you when I saw all the flowers.

The Pan American airlines are based here on Treasure island. Clipper ships are coming and going all the time. I had a good time on liberty last night. I saw a good show, had a steak dinner and went to a U.S.O. dance.

I saw a swell sight last night just as the sun was setting. My buddy and I were standing on the Golden Gate bridge when a few Destroyers sailed out into the Pacific. We seen them a lot but it sure was a sight to see them sail into the sun. I dont suppose it will be long before we'll be doing the same thing on some ship. But it will sure be a happy day when all the boys come back under the Golden Gate which we hope wont be long. Well Rose I guess we sounded off enough for today so till tomorrow. Love to all

Jim

29

June 11, 1944
Sunday afternoon

Dear Rose & All,

Good afternoon Mrs. Cook how's everything with you? I went to Mass in the chapel here on the base this morning. They have creeping bent grass growing around it and a lot of different flowers growing. I wish you could see it. I thought of you when I saw all the flowers.

The Pan American airlines are located here on Treasure Island. Clipper ships are coming and going all the time. I had a good time on liberty last night. I saw a good show, had a steak dinner and went to a U.S.O. dance.

I saw a swell sight last night just as the sun was setting. My buddy and I were standing on the Golden Gate bridge when a few Destroyers sailed out into the Pacific. I've seen them a lot but it sure was a sight to see them sail into the sun. I don't suppose it will be long before we'll be doing the same thing on some ship. But it will sure be a happy day when all the boys come back under the Golden Gate which we hope won't be too long. Well Rose I guess I've sounded off enough for today so till tomorrow,

Love to All,

Jim.

UNITED STATES NAVY

June 13, 1944

Dear Roses + all

Well here I am moved again.
They moved us right into the heart
of downtown Frisco. The place where
we stay was formely a hotel. I
didn't get a chance to write you
yesterday cause we were moving. I'm
on S.P. duty (Shore Patrol). Its the
same thing as Military Police in the
army. I have 8 hours on the beat
and 40 off. I don't know why
they picked me for this but
I'll be on it till we leave. I had
my first patrol today and I'm
sure tired, we walk around in
twos. I don't like it a bit
cause you have to carry out
regulations in regards to uniform
and see that everyone salutes. also
pick up drunk swabbies and
break up fights. Its a dirty
job and I don't like it. I tried
to talk my way out of it but
they stuck me on it.

2

The only thing I like about it is
our quarters. There really nice and
we have great big full length lockers.
They told me I'd probably be on
it a couple weeks. All sure be
glad when its over, cause I hate to
be a dam cop to the guys. I
have a hard time keeping myself
out of trouble without trying to keep
some one else out of it.

Hows everything at home?
I don't suppose my mail will
ever catch up with me.
I hope their through moving me
around so much. I'll sign off
now and hit the sack.

Love to all
Jim

P.S. New address is on envelope

31

June 13, 1944

Dear Rose & All,

Well here I am moved again. They moved us right into the heart of downtown Frisco. The place where we stay was formerly a hotel. I didn't get a chance to write you yesterday because we were moving. I'm on S.P. duty (Shore Patrol). It's the same thing as Military Police in the Army. I have 8 hours on the beat and 40 off. I don't know why they picked me for this but I'll be on it till we leave. I had my first patrol today and I'm sure tired, we walk around in two's. I don't like it a bit 'cause you have to carry out regulations in regards to uniform and see that everyone salutes. Also pick up drunk swabbies and break up fights. It's a dirty job and I don't like it. I tried to talk my way out of it but they stuck me on it.

The only thing I like about it is our quarters. They're really nice and we have great big full length lockers. They told me I'd probably be on it a couple weeks. I'll sure be glad when it's over, 'cause I hate to be a darn cop to the guys. I have a hard time keeping myself out of trouble without trying to keep someone else out of it.

How's everything at home? I don't suppose my mail will ever catch up with me. I hope they're through moving me around so much. I'll sign off now and hit the sack.

Love to all,

Jim

P.S. New address is on envelope

June 18th, 1944
Sunday Night

Dear Rose & all

Your voices all sounded swell on the phone today, I wish we could have talked a little longer but the telephone lines are jammed I guess. Tomorrow were suppose to get our physical and some shots in the arm. I kind of dread one of em, they say it really knocks a guy for a loop. Oh well, if it knocks me for a loop I wont have to work thats one consolation. ha ha.

Rose were going to get a marine issue of clothing and equipment so.

Were being assigned to the —— 8th & Art. You have nothing to worry about cause according to the info they gave us were being sent as replacements for some of these poor guys that have been out there for two years or more. I have a general idea of where will end up and its really hard for me to keep it to myself because I know you want to know. But if the censor will pass it I'll try and tell you as soon as we reach our destination. O.K.?

I think those cookies you sent

ought to be in the post office tomorrow, in fact I'm pretty sure they will be. Boy I'm really going to miss getting that swell box once a week, but I'll make up for it's when this is over.

Has Martie heard anything from Vince since D-Day? I hope she has. I'm sure he'll come through O.K. —— if he's still going now. Well Rose I'm getting a little tired so I guess I'll get a little sleep. Say Hi to everybody for me.

Love to all
Jim

(over)

P.S. We may have to send some of our clothing or bedding home so if you get some you'll know why.

June 18, 1944
Sunday Night

Dear Rose & All,

Your voices all sounded swell on the phone today. I wish we could have talked a little longer but the telephone lines are jammed I guess. Tomorrow we're supposed to get our physical and some shots in the arm. I kind of dread one of 'em, they say it really knocks a guy for a loop. Oh well if it knocks me for a loop I won't have to work that's one consolation. Ha ha.

Rose we're going to get a Marine issue of clothing and equipment too. We're being assigned to the 7th Fleet. You have nothing to worry about 'cause according to the info they gave us we're being sent as replacements for some of those poor guys that have been out there for two years or more. I have a general idea of where we'll end up and it's really hard for me to keep it to myself because I know you want to know. But if the censor will pass it I'll try and tell you as soon as we reach our destination, O.K.?

I think those cookies you sent ought to be in the post office tomorrow. In fact I'm pretty sure they will be. Boy I'm really going to miss getting that swell box once a week, but I'll make up for it when this is over.

Has Mrs. Etue heard anything from Funce since D-Day? I hope she has! I'm sure he'll come through O.K. if he's still going now. Well Rose I'm getting a little tired so I guess I'll get a little sleep. Say "Hi" to everybody for me.

Love to all,

Jim

P.S. We may have to send some of our clothing or bedding home so if you get some you'll know why.

34

June 19th, 1944

Dear Dad,

Sorry I haven't written you for so long, but I guess you know about me anyways, my letters to Rose. As you probably know already, we're leaving for overseas some time this week. I can't tell you much about it except that you won't have anything to worry about. You said if there was anything I wanted you to do for me to let you know. Well there is one thing and it will help me more than anything

else you could do. I wish you would remember me when you go to Mass and offer a Communion for me once in a while too. That's all I'll need, the Navy will take care of the material end of things. They're issuing marine clothing and gear to us, so you ought to be able to figure what kind of duty we'll have.

How are things running at the Shop? Rose tells me you're working regularly and that you're as busy as ever. I suppose the income tax takes a big

chunk out of your pay check, but we won't worry. We had quite a bit of trouble getting certain tools. I'll bet you could have fixed them up in a bit of it. But one thing is certain where we're going we'll have all the tools we need.

This Frisco is quite a place. There are a lot of pretty sights to see. Maybe after the war is over we could all take a trip and you could see some of them.

Time is running short so I'll sign off. Will drop a line as soon as I can.

So Long
Your Son
Jim

June 19, 1944

Dear Dad,

Sorry I haven't written you for so long, but I guess you heard about me through my letters to Rose. As you probably know already, we're leaving for overseas some time this week. I can't tell you much about it except that you won't have anything to worry about. You said if there was anything I wanted you to do for me to let you know.

Well there is one thing and it will help me more than anything else you could do. I wish you would remember me when you go to Mass and offer a Communion for me once in a while too. That's all I'll need, the Navy will take care of the material end of things. They're issuing Marine clothing and gear to us, so you ought to be able to figure what kind of duty we'll have.

How are things coming at the shop – Rose tells me you're working regularly and that you're as spry as ever. I suppose the income tax knocks a big chunk out of your pay check.

While I was at San Diego we had quite a bit of trouble getting certain tools. I'll bet you could have fixed them up in a hurry, eh? But one thing is certain where we're going we'll have all the tools we need.

This Frisco is quite a place. There are a lot of pretty sights to see. Maybe after the war is over we could all take a trip and you could see some of them.

Time is growing short so I'll sign off. I'll drop a line as soon as I can.
So Long

Your Son,
Jim.

Arriving in Milne Bay, New Guinea, aboard the U.S.S. Ward
which was the ship that fired the first shot of the war
against the Japanese in Pearl Harbor. U.S.S. Ward was sunk
by Japanese Kamikazes one month later.

July 14, 1944

Dear Cookie,

Hello Bummer, how's the world treating ya? I'll bet you're really getting a lot of fishing done. I'm in New Guinea now waiting assignment to a permanent station. It's winter here now but in between rains it's still hot as hell. I'm beginning to see why a lot of us guys get homesick. We had a nice trip over, good weather most of the way. It was a troop ship so I don't think I could tell you anything you haven't experienced yourself. When this thing is over some of the things I've got will come in handy for up north. I hope that day isn't too far away. This is about all I have to say today. I'll drop you a line the next chance I get. Be good and take it easy!

Jim

Hollandia Beach - New Guinea 1944

Page 3rd

Dear Rose & all

Sorry its taken me so long to write, but this is the first chance we had. I'm some where in New Guinea. Its winter here, but its still plenty hot and it rains a lot. A pair of hip boots would be just about right for the mud here. We have to take atrabine pills once a day, some fun. We were issued bed netting and head netting along with canteen, mess kit, and marine clothing.

I came over on a new troop ship

Behan - Bill - Bradley

Page Two

The weather was nice most of the way, so hardly anyone got sick. I'm not going to be stationed here permanently. This is a receiving station and I'll be assigned to some where from here. When you write please send it air mail, because ordinary mail takes forever and a day to get here. I'll sign off now. Say hello to everybody for me.

Love to all

Jim

July 14, 1944

Dear Rose & All,

Sorry it's taken me so long to write but this is the first chance I've had. I'm somewhere in New Guinea. It's winter here, but it's still plenty hot and it rains a lot. A pair of hip boots would be just about right for the mud here. We have to take atropine pills once a day, some fun. We were issued bed netting and head netting along with canteen, mess kit, and Marine clothing.

I came over on a new troop ship. The weather was nice most of the way, so hardly anyone got sick. I'm not going to be stationed here permanently. This is a receiving station and I'll be assigned to somewhere from here. When you write please sent it Air Mail, because ordinary mail takes forever and a day to get here. I'll sign off for now. Say hello to everybody for me.

Love to All,

Jim.

The Japanese had attacked and taken control of New Guinea in February of 1942 because it was centrally located near Japan, the Philippines and Australia. That war campaign, which began almost immediately after the occupation, has since been all but forgotten except by those who served there.

Led by General Douglas MacArthur, the United States and its Allies completed the liberation of New Guinea from the Japanese in 1945.

It's been reported that the New Guinea campaign had Allied casualties numbering over 127,000.

Dear Irish,

No I haven't forgotten you, this is the first chance I've had to drop you a line. In a little while I'm going to Mass. That's one thing I'm thankful for, that we have Mass here every Sunday morning. We use a small platform and some coconut logs for a church. St. John's would look like a Cathedral to me now. Did melban (not sure this is correct) come to Flint to spend part of the summer with you yet? By the time this gets to you over half your vacation will be over. I'll bet you have been having some swell times. I sure envy you. How are you and Fr. Flannigan & Fr. Burns coming? Say hello to them for me and write soon.

Your Bro & Pal

Jim

1944 Pocket Calendar he used to write notes about where he was.

"Left USA June 23, 1944

Arrived Milne Bay New Guinea 7-14-44

Crossed Equator June 30, 1944"

James Behan TM3c
313-27-30

Somewhere In
New Guinea
July 17, 1944

AMERICAN RED CROSS

Dear Rose & all

Good morning, hows all the gang? fine I hope. I went to mass for all of you yesterday. I also went to confession and would have gone to communion if I hadn't broke my 4 hour fast from solids by going to chow. I'll make up for it next Sunday. Yesterday I was too hungry.

Right now its raining cats & dogs, but I suppose the sun will be out in a few minutes. Thats the way the weather runs here.

Has Mrs. Otre heard anything from Gunce since the invasion? How about Joe Austin's son, have they sent him home yet, or is he still over here?

Balle - Behan - Moss - Berg

TORPEDO CREW - USS DOBBIN + ME

#2

James Behan TM3c
313-27-30

AMERICAN RED CROSS

I have a little money and I was planning on sending it home when I got here, but we dont get payed while were here so I think I'll wait until the next time I get payed and send the whole works home. I ought to have a pretty good pay next time.

I haven't much more to say. They wont let us tell anything so there isn't much to write about. I'm o.k. so dont worry about me. Probably safer here than you are, with all those dizzy drivers around here. ha ha

Please write and let me know how much their cutting out of my letters.

Love to all
Jim

43

James Behan TM3C
313-27-30

Dear Rose & All

Good Morning, how's all the gang?, fine I hope. I went to Mass for all of you yesterday. I also went to confession and would have gone to Communion if I hadn't broke my 4 hour fast from solids by going to chow. I'll make up for it next Sunday. Yesterday I was too hungry.

Right now it's raining cats & dogs, but I suppose the sun will be out in a few minutes. That's the way the weather runs here.

Has Mrs. Etue heard anything from Funce since the invasion? How about Joe Austin's son, have they sent him home yet, or is he still over here?

I have a little money and I was planning on sending it home when I got here, but we don't get paid while we're here so I think I'll wait until the next time I get paid and send the whole works home. I ought to have a pretty good pay next time.

I haven't much more to say. They won't let us tell anything so there isn't much to write about. I'm O.K. so don't worry about me. Probably safer than you are with all those dizzy drivers around home ha ha.

Please write and let me know how much they're cutting out of my letters.

Love to All,

Jim

To
MRS. FRANK COOK
418 Dougherty Place
FLINT 4, MICHIGAN

From 313-27-30
JAMES BROWN Mpc
R/13 NAVY 467
% Fleet Post Office
SAN FRANCISCO, Calif
July 24 1944

Somewhere in the Pacific

Dear Rose & All

I'm very happy tonight because I just received an air mail letter that you wrote June 20th. Rose I don't think I ever appreciated a letter so much before in my life. I must have read it ten times already. They say there is some more mail coming in from the states tomorrow so I'm in hopes of getting another. Tell Bobby to take it easy working at Amadys, these slave drivers and he could easily hurt himself. I'm glad to hear Mike got such a good job. I'll drop you a line again the very next chance I get.

Love to all
Jim

V---MAIL

July 21, 1944
Somewhere in New Guinea

Dear Rose & All

I'm very happy tonight because I just received an air mail letter that you wrote June 20th. Rose I don't think I ever appreciated a letter so much before in my life. I must have read it ten times already. They say there is some more mail coming in from the states tomorrow so I'm in hopes of getting another. Tell Bobby to take it easy working at Hamadys, they're slave drivers and he could easily hurt himself. I'm happy to hear Mike (Dad's cousin) got such a good job. I'll drop you a line again the very next chance I get.

Love to All

Jim

Joe Becker & Myself on 3" A.A. Gun

James Behan M2c   August 6, 1944
                                    New Guinea
                                    Sunday afternoon

Dear Rose & All

        Hi toots, whats cookin? I can
almost smell that roast beef dinner
that your having today. Today we were
extremely lucky and had meat loaf, mashed
potatoes, asparagus, corn, bread & butter, ice
tea, and pumpkin pie. That was the
best chow we've had since I remember.
Everything tasted swell because we've been
living off Spam & Vienna sausage.

        Jack Benny and his show
did come here Friday night. He
brought Lanny Ross, Carol Landis, Martha
Tilton and a few others. They put
on a swell show and even the
bluest guys around had to laugh.

James Behan M2c   2

        Yesterday I started working in the
Post Office, I'm going to work there until
I leave this place. While I was working
I was sitting, I found some, ... to buy stationery,
Oh gay a use to run around with, you knowing
I really do want this because it's very
old ... I will write him a little note
... the ... to say.

        We've had surprisingly good
weather for a day and a half, but it
looks like it will break loose any minute
boy what a rackett, an umbrella man
would have in this joint.

        I haven't had any mail for three
days but when the mail does come
through I'll be first to get it. That's
what I like about working at the P.O.

James Behan M2c   3

        also by working there it makes the time
go fast, which is very important here.

        I couldn't go to Mass this
morning but I'm going this afternoon
at 4:00 o'clock. They have a special
Mass in the afternoon for those who
have to work Sunday morning.

        This is about all the news
I have right now. Don't work too
hard, tell pappy I'm O.K.

                        Love to All
                        Jim

James Behan TM3C

Dear Rose & All

Hi Ozie, what's cookin? I can almost smell that roast beef dinner that you're having today. Today we were extremely lucky and had Meat loaf, mashed potatoes, asparagus, corn, bread & butter, ice tea, and pumpkin pie. That was the best chow I've had since I came here. Everything tasted swell because we've been living off Spam & Vienna sausage.

Jack Benny and his show did come last Friday night. He brought Lanny Ross, Carol Landis, Martha Tilden and a few others. They put on a swell show and even the blueist guys in the crowd had to laugh.

Yesterday I started working in the Post Office. I'm going to work there until I leave this place. While I was sorting some letters I found some addressed to Jack Chatterson (the guy I used to run around with, you know him). Evidently he isn't here because it's very old mail. I wrote him a little note on the back of the envelope.

We've had surprisingly good weather for a day and a half, but it looks like it will break loose any minute. Boy what a racket an umbrella man would have in this joint.

I haven't had any mail for three days but when the mail does come through I'll be first to get it. That's what I like about working at the P.O. Also by working there it makes the time go fast, which is very important here.

I couldn't go to Mass this morning but I'm going this afternoon at 4:00 O'clock. They have a special Mass in the afternoon for those who have to work Sunday morning.

This is about all the news I have right now. Don't work too hard, tell pappy I'm O.K.

Love to All,
Jim

ROBERT "IRISH" RENNE
4R DOUGHERTY PLACE
FLINT, 4, MICHIGAN

James _____
R/a Navy 147
c/o Fleet Post Office
San Francisco
August 7, 1944

Milne Bay New Guinea

Dear Irish,

During the past week I have received two letters from you dated June 4th + 13th. Even though they ___ are a couple months old I was very glad to hear from you. By the time you get this you will probably be looking forward to going back to school again. I hope you've had a good time this summer. From what Rose said you've been doing a lot of work along with the fun. Maybe next time you're home for the summer I won't have to write to you. Say hello to Fr. _____ + Anne for me.

Yours ___ + Pal
Jim

Dear Irish;

During the past week I have received two letters from you dated June 4th & 13th. Even though they are a couple months old I was very glad to hear from you. By the time you get this you will probably be looking forward to going back to school again.

I hope you've had a good time this summer. From what Rose said you've been doing a lot of work along with the fun. Maybe next time you're home for the summer I won't have to write to you.

Say hello to Fr. Flanigan & Bums for me

Your Bro & Pal,

Jim.

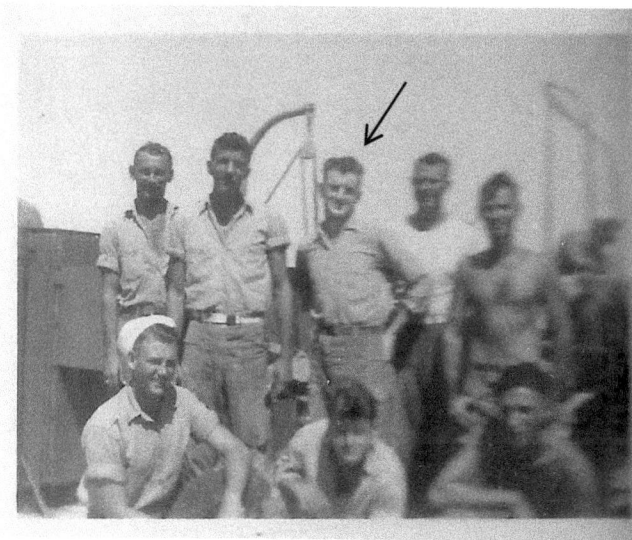

Dad & his ship mates left the U.S.S. Ward and spent 3 days and nights camped on the beach at the jungle's edge in New Guinea. He told us how it was a very miserable experience. He said it was muddy, hot, lots of nasty insects and snakes. They were very relieved when the U.S.S. Dobbin finally arrived to head to the Philippines.

No.

MRS. FANNY COOK
418 Dougherty Place
Flint, Michigan

James Bohan TM2c
[Sender's name]

A/S Navy 169 ⅟₀ F.P.O.
[Ship address]

San Francisco, Calif.

14 August 1944
[Date]

New Guinea

Dear Rose & all,

Today I received your V-mail letter of July 31st. Thanks for sending me a copy of Frances letter, I'll write him the first chance I get. Rose you asked me to tell you if there is anything I need, I wish you would send me a pack of light air mail paper, just the paper, no envelopes. Like the kind that I write my air mail letters to you on, I can't get anymore, and my supply is running low. Tell Patsy, I received her letter and to send the box of candy whenever she wants to. Tell her not to send any soft stuff, because it will melt crossing the equator. They don't censor your letters so don't be afraid to tell me anything you want to. This is all for now

Love to all
Jim

V—MAIL

51

14, August, 1944
New Guinea

Dear Rose & All

Today I received your Vmail letter of July 31st. Thanks for sending me a copy of Funce's letter I'll write him the first chance I get. Rose you asked me to tell you if there is anything I need. I wish you would send me a pack of light air mail paper, just the paper, no envelopes. Like the kind that I write my air mail letters to you on. I can't get any more and my supply is running low. Tell Patsy I received her letter and to send the box of candy when she wants to. Tell her not to send any soft stuff because it will melt crossing the equator. They don't censor your letters so don't be afraid to tell me anything you want to. This is all for now.

Love to All

Jim

Dad told us of how most of the guys on the ship had gotten a bad case of dysentery from the camping excursion. Severe diarrhea forced the men to spend a lot of time in the latrines, which were made up of a long bench-style bank of "holes" along a wall. When the seas got rough and the ship swayed, they had to stand up at strategic times in order to keep from being "splashed" on.

To
MR. ROBERT BEHAN
420 COTTAGE GROVE
FLINT, MICHIGAN

From
James Robert Behan
R/m Navy 169 ℅ P.O.
San Francisco, Calif.
23. August 1944

Dear Dad   ~~[censored]~~ New Guinea

I have a few spare minutes so I thought I'd drop you a line to let you know I'm okay and I hope your the same. There's not much to say that I haven't already told you. When I first got here it rained quite a bit but lately it has been pretty dry and hot. I expect to be moved at any time I don't know where or what I'll be assigned to yet, but I hope it's a ship. Dad did you do what I asked you to just before I left the States? That's all I really need and it will help me more than anything else. I hope by next year at this time I will either be home or back in the States. I think the first time I hit Frisco I could run the rest of the way home. This is all I have to say right now so I'll close. Don't work too ~~hard~~ and write when you can.

Jim

23, August, 1944
New Guinea

Dear Dad

I have a few spare minutes so I thought I'd drop you a line to let you know I'm okay and I hope you're the same. There's not much to say that I haven't already told you. When I first got here it rained quite a bit but lately it has been pretty dry and hot. I expect to be moved at any time. I don't know where or what I'll be assigned to yet, but I hope it's a ship. Dad did you do what I asked you to just before I left the States? (He asked his dad to go to Mass and offer a Communion for him) That's all I really need and it will help me more than anything else. I hope by next year at this time I will either be home or back in the States. I think the first time I hit Frisco I could run the rest of the way home.

This is all I have to say right now so I'll close. Don't work too hard and write when you can.

Jim

Sept 3, 1944
U.S.S. Dolphin
Somewhere in S.W.P.

Dear Rose & all

Im aboard ship now and you will find my correct address on the envelope. The chow is good, we can have all we want, Im going to make up for a little Ive missed. We have movies whenever were in port. I can't tell you much about the ship except that its big. We have ice cream to buy about 4 nights a week. There is plenty of soap, tooth paste & so on. This probably don't sound like much to you but out here its considered a good deal. Its very hot here now but I have tanned quite a bit so I don't have to worry about sun burn.

2

Rose you won't have to worry about me because on this ship Im as safe as you can be out here. The work is hard and theirs plenty of it but when a guy gets chow like we do he doesn't mind work. This address will be for the duration so when you send mail or boxes I'll get them direct. Rose you wanted to send me something, will when you do make sure it is wrapped good and won't melt otherwise it won't get to me. This is all for tonight. Im kind of tired so I'll close. Say hello to all for me.

Love to all
Jim

Sept 3, 1944
U.S.S. Dobbin
Somewhere in S.W.P.

Dear Rose & All

I'm aboard ship now and you will find my correct address on the envelope. The chow is good, we can have all we want, so I'm going to make up for a little I've missed. We have movies whenever we're in port. I can't tell you much about the ship except that it's big. We have ice cream to buy about 4 nights a week. There is plenty of soap, toothpaste and so on. This probably don't sound like much to you but out here it's considered a good deal. It's very hot here now but I have tanned quite a bit so I don't have to worry about sun burn.

Rose you won't have to worry about me because on this ship I'm as safe as you can be out here. The work is hard and there's plenty of it but when a guy gets chow like we do he doesn't mind work. This address will be for the duration so when you send mail or boxes I'll get them direct. Rose you wanted to send something – well when you do make sure it is wrapped good and won't melt otherwise it won't get to me.

This is all for tonight. I'm kind of tired so I'll close. Say hello to all for me.

Love to All

Jim

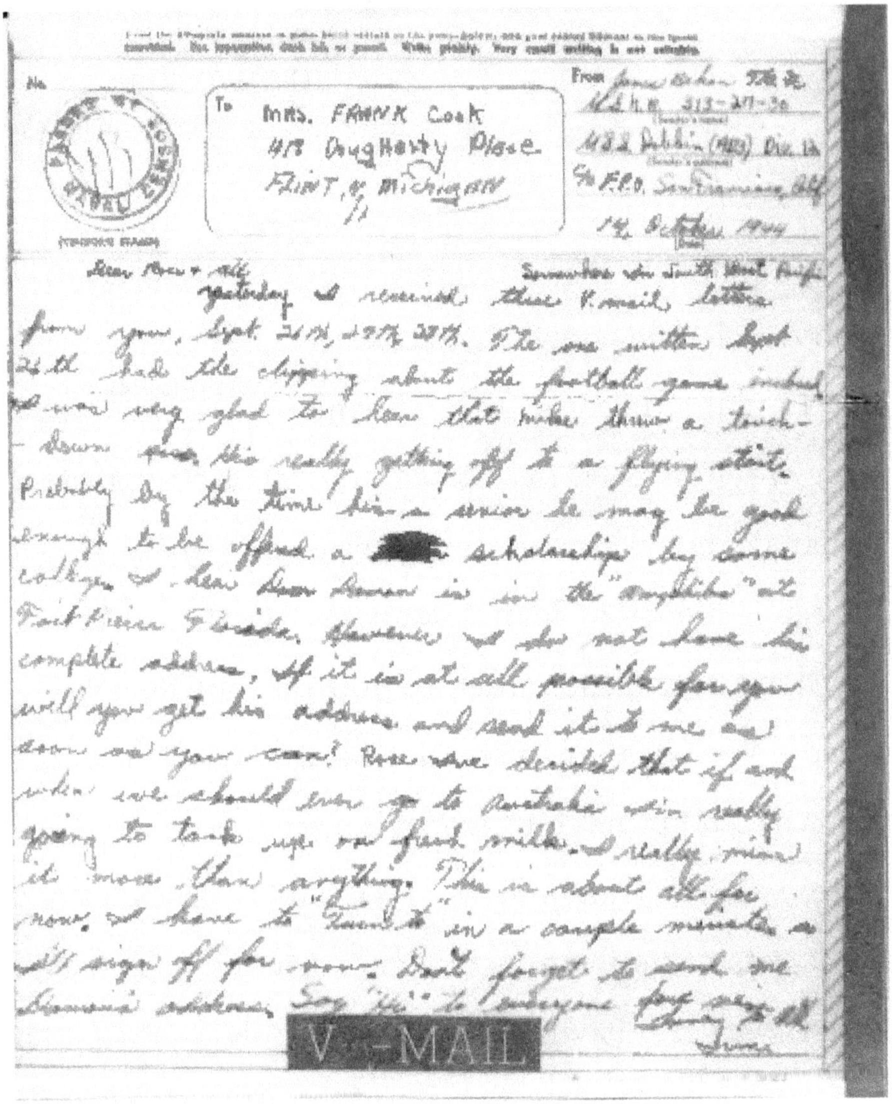

To MRS. FRANK Cook
418 Dougherty Place
FLINT, Michigan

From [illegible]
c/o F.P.O. San Francisco, Calif.
14 October 1944

Dear Mom + all, Somewhere in South West Pacific

Yesterday I received three V-mail letters from you, Sept. 21st, 24th, 27th. The one written Sept 26th had the clipping about the football game indeed I was very glad to hear that Mike threw a touch-down. He's really getting off to a flying start. Probably by the time he's a senior he may be good enough to be offered a [redacted] scholarship by some college. I hear [illegible] is in the "amphibs" at Fort Pierce Florida. However I do not have his complete address. If it is at all possible for you will you get his address and send it to me as soon as you can! Rose we decided that if and when we should ever go to Australia we're really going to take up on fresh milk. I really miss it more than anything. This is about all for now. I have to "turn to" in a couple minutes so I'll sign off for now. Don't forget to send me [illegible] address. Say "Hi" to everyone for me. Love to all

[illegible]

V-MAIL

Destroyers alongside

14, October, 1944
Somewhere in South West Pacific

Dear Rose & All

Yesterday I received these Vmail letters from you; Sept. 26th, 27th, 28th. The one written Sept. 26th had the clipping about the football game included. I was very glad to hear that Mike threw a touchdown pass. He's really getting off to a flying start. Probably by the time he's a senior he may be good enough to be offered a scholarship by some colleges. I hear <u>Dean Damon</u> (not sure this is correct) is in the "Amphibs" at Fort Pierce Florida. However I do not have his complete address. If it is at all possible for you will you get his address and send it to me as soon as you can? Rose I've decided that if and when we should ever go to Australia I'm really going to tank up on fresh milk. I really miss it more than anything. This is about all for now. I have to "Turn to" in a couple minutes so I'll sign off for now. Don't forget to send me <u>Daman's</u> (not sure this is correct) address. Say "Hi" to everyone for me.

Love to All

Jim

UNITED STATES NAVY

23, October, 1944
(No 6¢ stamps available)

Dear Rose & all

Today I received your air mail letters of the 11th and 13th. Your mail has been coming through right on the dot lately. Gosh Rose from what you say about all the boxes that are being sent to me they'll have to open a branch Post Office for me alone, ha ha. You inquired as to what kind of a razor I have. Well Rose its just an ordinary double edge safety razor. I paid 35¢ for it at Norfolk and have been using it ever since. Any double edge blade will fit it. We don't have much trouble getting blades, but good ones are scarce. So if you send me some I'll be able to use them. There is one thing I can always use. Is the old Burn in still up north, maybe he's turning into a hermit eh?

I suppose you have been worrying about me when ___
___ and that ___

This portion was cut out with scissors.

So I'll tell you there's nothing to worry about, everything is going okay. I can't tell you what I want to, if I could I'm sure I could put your mind as to what I'm doing and you wouldn't worry.

Rose there is something else I want to tell

Roy Berg in Catacombs 1944

Torpedo in Catacombs

.2

UNITED STATES NAVY

you, and that is you don't have to worry about me catching cold. Even tho its hot the whole year around. The only time I wear a shirt is at night when it gets a little cooler and breezy. Last night I saw a good comedy named "Two Girls & a Sailor". Its about the latest picture I've seen. My friend Sheppard thinks he will be leaving for the states soon. We thought he would be gone by now but you know how much you can plan ahead in the Navy. However I'll let you know as soon as he leaves. He said he will be sure and drop in on you when he gets home. Gibis is about all I can think of to say right now. Thanks for the swell letters. Say Hello to Dad for me.

Love to all
Jim

James Behan TM 3/c

23, October, 1944

Dear Rose & All

Today I received your Air mail letters of the 12th and 13th. Your mail has been coming through on the dot lately. Gosh Rose from what you say about all the boxes that are being sent to me they'll have to open a branch Post Office for me alone, ha ha. You inquired as to what kind of a razor I have. Well Rose it's just an ordinary double edge safety razor. I paid .35¢ for it at Norfolk and have been using it ever since. Any double edge blade will fit it. We don't have much trouble getting blades, but good ones are scarce. So if you send me some I'll be able to use them, they're one thing I can always use.
So the ole bum is still up north, maybe he's turning into a hermit eh?

I suppose you have been worrying about me when, (Censored Material) and that, (Censored) to tell you there's nothing to worry about, everything is going okay. I can't tell you what I want to, if I could I'm sure I could put you wise as to what I'm doing and you wouldn't worry.

Rose there is something else I want to tell you and that is you don't have to worry about me catching cold. Over here it's hot the whole year around. The only time I wear a shirt is at night when it gets a little cooler and breezy. Last night I saw a good comedy named "Two Girls & a Sailor". It's about the latest picture I've seen. My friend Sheppard thinks he will be leaving for the States soon. He thought he would be gone by now but you know how much you can plan ahead in the Navy. However I'll let you know as soon as he leaves. He said he will be sure and drop in on you when he gets home. This is about all I can think of to say right now. Thanks for the swell letters. Say Hello to Dad for me.

Love to All

Jim

James Behan T.M. 3/c

60

Dear Rose & all

Last night I received two boxes. One from Patsy, with the things you sent me for my birthday and the other which you sent with Mrs. Otis' cookies & cake. Rose I can't begin to tell you how pleased I am with the sandals and shaving kit. Their just what's needed and wanted most. That polishing cloth for shoes is really a pip, works swell. The sandals arrived just in time to save my dogs. Out here when I wear shoes the heat makes my feet blister and crack, so you can see how handy the sandals will be. I'm going to write Mrs. Otis some time today and thank her for the things she sent. Another thing that came just in time was the sewing kit. I sew my name in all my clothes and I run out of both needles and thread. You couldn't have sent anything that I needed

Tub Bath

more than what you did send. All I can say is Thanks a million.

I received a letter from Bobby written in Petaluma yesterday. Rose when he's home for Christmas please ask him to send his letters air mail from now on instead of 3¢. Airmail on the whole is faster than V mail or anything.

There is a scorching hot morning. I woke up and it felt like that ball of fire had crawled in bed with me. Probably when I do come home my blood will be so thin I'll freeze to death. This will be all for now as I haven't any time left. Thanks again for everything. Say hello to everyone for me.

Tell Jackie & Patsy Thanks too.
Love to All
Jim

James _____ F.M.3c

Fix 'em Fish

19/12/44
Tuesday Morning

Dear Rose & All

Last night I received two boxes. One from Patsy with the things you sent me for my birthday and the other which you sent with Mrs. Etue's cookies & cake. Rose I can't begin to tell you how pleased I am with the sandals and shaving kit. They're just what I needed and wanted most. That polishing cloth for shoes is really a pip, works swell. The sandals arrived just in time to save my dogs. Out here when I wear shoes the heat makes my feet blister and crack, so you can see how handy the sandals will be. I'm going to write Mrs. Etue sometime today and thank her for the things she sent. Another thing that came just in time was the sewing kit. I sew my name in all my clothes and I'd run out of both needles and thread. You couldn't have sent anything that I needed more than what you did send. All I can say is Thanks a million.

I received a letter from Bobby written in October yesterday. Rose when he's home for Christmas please ask him to send his letters air mail from now on instead of 3¢. Air mail in the whole is faster than Vmail or anything.

This is a scorching hot morning. I woke up and it felt like that ball of fire had crawled in bed with me. Probably when I do come home my blood will be so thin I'll freeze to death. This will be all for now as I haven't any time left. Thanks again for everything. Say hello to everyone for me.
Tell Cookie & Patsy Thanks too.

Love to All
Jim
James Behan T.M.3/c

Stormy Weather

Stormy Weather

Note the Navy Censor Removed one photo

Dear Cookie:

Hello Bum, I received several letters from Rose yesterday one with your letter enclosed. I also got the Christmas card and the dollar. Yesterday they had me going hot for 20 hours so today they gave me a little time off to crap out. I can't sleep because it's too hot so I thought now would be a good time to do a little writing. I hope you sold all your 1200 Christmas trees, Boy what I'd give to see one with a little snow on it right now. They say that a guy eventually gets use to this climate, but I don't think I ever will. I've got some of that darn heat rash and boy does it drive me nuts. Tell Rose not to worry about it, about 50 per cent of the guys get it. I have another 12 months to go before I can put my chit in for rehabilitation leave and new construction. The way things look we'll still have plenty of war to fight next year at this time. I'm beginning to think we will have the Japs pretty well done up by the time they get through with Germany, the news from Europe doesn't sound good.

We had a pretty good Christmas dinner and I suppose it will be Easter before we get another one like it. Tokyo Rose made a broadcast and said she was going to bomb us on Christmas day but I guess Rosie changed her mind. One of the guys on the ship got a hold of some pictures of the natives of places we've been. He gave me some so I'm enclosing a few, hope Irish isn't shocked by that little bugger who believes in southern exposure. Say Hello to Danny & Baby Sister and all the kids for me. Tell Baby Sister thanks for dropping me a line. I almost forgot to mention that I received a Vmail from Pat Goggins, tell Pat thanks for writing. I think I'd better close now, I'm getting sleepy and I think I'll make it this time heat or no heat. There are five pictures, let me know if you get 'em.

So Long for now

Jim

James Behan T.M. 3/c

> Note: Dad said there were five pictures but the Navy censors removed one.

Transferring Torpedo

Jan 11, 1945

Dear Rose & All,

I've sure received a lot of mail from all of you in the last few days. There is three regular mail and three Vmail and also Patsy's Christmas card & spiritual bouquet. I'm glad you liked the presents and that you did get an antique vase for yourself, as I know that's what you like most. Bobby sent me a rosary for Christmas. I can use it because my other one got broke and I lost it. I'm going to write him as soon as I can. Gee Rose I wish I could feel some of that snow you're all talking about. I'll never gripe about cold weather again as long as I live.

We've been awful busy so I haven't had much time to write lately. I don't want you to worry about me because nothing's going to happen to me on this old work horse.

So Clem has another one on the way eh? Right in there pitching isn't he, O well. I hope everything turns out okay. By the way are the Herricks on Frank St. still going full blast?

How's that bum husband of yourn? Does he still sleep till 11 o'clock on Sunday, get up go to church, come back and sit on the stool the rest of the day? I can't say that I blame him. I'm going to do a little of the same when I get drafted back into civies.

Say hi to everyone and thank Patsy for the spiritual bouquet. So long for now.

Love to All
Jim

James Behan T.M. 3/c

Feb. 8, 1945
U.S.S. ...

Dear Mother,

I guess it has been a week or more since I last wrote, but the Senator and his ...

I can't tell you where we are going now, but I'll write you ...

... so much luck on the first try ...

Love to all,
Jim

Feb 18, 1945
U.S.S. Dobbin (Ad3)
Somewhere at Sea

Dear Rose & All,

       I believe it has been a week or more since the last time I wrote. During that time I have received two boxes of candy from you mailed from Saunders. Also I received five letters. The candy was a little soft from the heat but not enough to make any difference, it was swell thanks a lot. You people don't know how lucky you are to have all that nice cool snow, I sure envy you. So Funce Etue is in Belgium attached to an L.C.M. I wondered where he would end up, but I can't understand why they issued him Army gear unless he's waiting on the beach to pick up his ship.

       I can't tell you where we're going now but I'll give you 3 guesses.

Don't worry about me I'm okay. I have taken one roll of film and developed it. The negatives are swell but I've had a little trouble getting prints. However I'm fixing up a gismo that should bring them out swell. As soon as I get them the way I want 'em I'll send you some. My biggest problem is finding a dark room where some jerk won't be sticking his neck in and out every two minutes. I'm having a lot of fun with the set and it's really interesting. I really was surprised that I had so much luck for the first try.

Well Rose I guess I'd better sign off for now. Thanks for everything and say hello to everyone for me, Phillip too.

                          Love to All
                          Jim

James Behan T.M. 3/c

UNITED STATES NAVY

Censors cut this out

Duty "B" - Subic Bay, P.I. 1945

Myself & Ol Smith - Philippines 1945

UNITED STATES NAVY

tell me if the censor let you
know where I am.

Love to all
Gin

27, February, 1945
(Location cut out by censors)

Dear Rose & All,

I thought I was busy before but boy have we been goin' hot these last few days. I want you to know I'm okay, just haven't had any mail for about two weeks now but that's because the only way it comes in here is by ship. I've seen some historic spots and a few other things too. I'm going to get some pictures of these ports. I probably won't be able to mail them to you because of censorship regulations. However the war isn't going to last forever and I'll be home some day and show them to you then. One thing I like about it here is that it's cooler and I'm getting rid of my heat rash at last. I was beginning to think there wasn't any civilization on this side of the Pacific, but there is. Say Hi to everyone for me and write and tell me if the censor let you know where I am.

Love to all,

Jim

James Behan T.M. 3/c

"Red Lead" Row

Dear Cookie,

Hello you bum, received your gay hunk of correspondence yesterday, you sawed typist. Its about time you got on the ball and wrote me a letter but I suppose your like me. It seems like everytime I write home it gets a little harder. I have plenty to talk about but everytime I try to slip it through the censor rejects my letter. So I guess I'll just have to keep on with the same old line that you've been getting. I have some pictures developed and printed, and prob'ly taking one look at them its easy to tell that I'm a rank amateur. However I shall send a few home as soon as I can get around to it. I'm going to see if I can get permission to send some of the negatives home, as most of my trouble comes when I try to print them. I have

#2

a hell of a time trying to find a dark room. In two days I will have 9 months overseas. Thats just half the time I need before I can put in for rehabilitation leave. Usually after you have 9 months overseas they foolishly fiddle around for 4 to 6 months before you start home. So I figure I have about 1/3 of my time in. I suppose it was the same in the last war as it is in this. Its who you know not what you know. But I won't be in the Navy forever I hope. The fellow that I was telling you about that lives in Flint and was suppose to have gone home is still here. His time was up last September. Thats an example of how long I'll be over here if the war doesn't end. But I have nothing to gripe about, Perley's brother spent 3 years in over here before he got home.

#3

You know Mike Ryan that lives on Herbert St? Well, his son is on an L.S.T. and its about 1/3 a mile from me right now. I knew the number of it and I spotted it yesterday. Got a letter from old Bert Hamilton a couple days ago. He's on a P.C.E. (Patrol Craft Escort) We call em dehydrated frigates. From what I can make out he must be working up around the Aleutians. In one of his letters he said he had snow and ice for Christmas this year, so that must be where he is. I haven't heard from Francis Otis for quite a while. In his last letter he said he had been issued a full army pack and equipment so they must have made him a doggie. This will be all for today. Thanks for writing and write again soon.

Jim
alias "The Sissy"

JAMES BEHAN 7.9.8.

Behan looking at Corregidor

Booby trapped ammo magazine
One of ours died here

March 21, 1945

Dear Cookie,

Hello you bum; received your gay hunk of correspondence yesterday, your some typist. It's about time you got on the ball and wrote me a letter but I suppose you're like me. It seems like every time I write home it gets a little harder. I have plenty to talk about but every time I try to slip it through the censor rejects my letter. So I guess I'll just have to keep on with the same old line you've been getting. I have some pictures developed and printed, and just by taking one look at them it's easy to tell that I'm a rank amateur. However I shall send a few home as soon as I can get around to it. I'm going to see if I can get permission to send some of the negatives home, as most of my trouble comes when I try to print them. I have a hell of a time trying to find a dark room. In two days I will have 9 months overseas. That's just half the time I need before I can put in for rehabilitation leave. Usually after you have 18 months overseas they fool and fiddle around for 4 to 6 months before you start home. So I figure I have about 1/3 of my time in. I suppose it was the same in the last war is it is in this. It's who you know not what you know. But I won't be in the Navy forever, I hope. This fellow that I was telling you about that lives in Flint and was supposed to have gone home is still here. His time was up last September. That's an example of how long

I'll be over here if the war doesn't end. But I have nothing to gripe about. Teefey's (not sure of spelling) brother put 3 years in over here before he got home.

You know Mike Ryan that lives on Norbert St.? Well his son is on an L.S.T. and it's about 1/2 mile from me right now. I knew the number of it and I spotted it yesterday. Got a letter from old Bert Hamilton a couple days ago. He's on a P.C.E. (Patrol Craft Escort). We call 'em dehydrated frigates. As near as I can make out he must be working up around the Aleutians. In one of his letters he said he had snow and ice for Christmas this year, so that must be where he is. I haven't heard from Funce Etue for quite a while. In his last letter he said he had been issued a full Army pack and equipment so they must have made him a doggie. This will be all for today. Thanks for writing and write again soon.

Jim

Alias

"The Sissy"

James Behan TM 3/c

14" on Corregidor

USS Cleveland

USS Sperry – Sub Tender

Landing Craft Infantry Ship

USS Buck

Not labeled but 725 was

Destroyer USS O'Brien

Not labeled but 387 was

Submarine USS Pintado

USS Jenkins after hitting a mine-Subic

april 8, 1945

Dear Rose & all

Hello we have receiving your letters regularly but haven't had time to write to you. So Haley got hooked eh? He can have my share of it for a long time to come. After watching and listening to some of these "sad apples" commonly called "married men", I'm becoming a confirmed bachelor. I guess I told you the same thing once before didn't I? You asked me about my weight, well its 165. I guess the food is all right but I can tell what day of the week it is by what we have. Eating is just a habit! Thanks for the Easter card and the money. Maybe next year I'll be able to spend Easter in the promised land.

My friend Sheppard left for home a few days ago. I gave him your home & office address and he said

2

he would drop in and see you. I expect he will be home by the first of June. His name is Lionel Sheppard. Store Keeper 3/c. A week ago was Easter; I went to Mass & Communion for you and everyone at home. I hear from Rich about 2 or 3 times a month. He certainly is serious isn't he? Please excuse the pen & hope you will be able to make this out. I imagine Prince Ottie was in the "amphibs" that took the army across the Rhine, hope he came through all right. Say Hello to Mrs Ottie for me. Well this is all for now. So Long and be good! Love to All

Jim

Jas Bedan T.M. 3/c

Sunken Japs Manila Bay

April 8, 1945

Dear Rose & All,

Hello, I've been receiving your letters regularly but haven't had time to write you. So Haley got hooked eh? He can have my share of it for a long time to come. After watching and listening to some of these "sad apples" commonly called "married men", I'm becoming a confirmed bachelor. I guess I told you the same thing once before didn't I?

You asked me about my weight, well it's 165. I guess the food is all right but I can tell what day of the week it is by what we have. Eating is just a habit. Thanks for the Easter card and the money. Maybe next year I'll be able to spend Easter in the Promised Land.

My friend Sheppard left for home a few days ago. I gave him your home & office address and he said he would drop in and see you. I expect he will be home by the first of June. His name is Lionel Sheppard, Store Keeper 3/c. A week ago was Easter; I went to Mass & Communion for you and everyone at home. I hear from Irish about 2 or 3 times a month. He certainly is serious isn't he? Please excuse the pen, I hope you will be able to make this out. I imagine Funce Etue was in the "Amphibs" that took the Army across the Rhine, hope he came through all right. Say Hello to Mrs. Etue for me. This is all for now. So long and be good.

Love to all,

Jim

James Behan T.M. 3/c

Shot up '41 Plymouth
used by the Japs during
their occupation -Manila

Downtown Manila

Santo Tomas
Internment Camp

August 14, 1945
Tuesday Morning

August 14, 1945

Dear Rose & All,

Received your box with the fruit cake and two rolls of film. I was very surprised to get the film and I appreciate the trouble you took to get it. The cake is swell, nice and firm and tasty. It really is a treat Rose. Thanks a million.

I had hopes that by this time I would be sending you a five dollar money order for our bet. But it kinda looks like the rats have gotta be blown out of the hole. I was asleep when they put out the surrender offer. One of my buddies woke me and told me the war was over. I thought it was too good to be true and I guess it was. But maybe if they're "atomized" a little more the war will be over. Let's hope that by the time you receive this letter the runt on the white horse will have surrendered. Tomorrow would be a very appropriate day for it to end wouldn't it?

I am enclosing some pictures that were taken several months ago when we were in Manila. There are 8 all together. Another fellow had the negatives, so we got together and printed them.

I also received a couple letters from Patsy besides your mail. Tell her and Cookie I will write them soon. How is everyone at home? We are going to have Mass at 0615 tomorrow morning being that it is Aug. 15th. There is a lot of scuttlebutt about the Dobbin going Stateside. I don't put much stock in it though, because I've heard it ever since I came aboard. Anyway it's nice to think about.

What do you think about the atom bomb? It has tremendous possibilities but then if it should ever get into the wrong hands the world wouldn't be a safe place to live. You can imagine what would have happened if the Germans had won the race to develop the atom bomb. If it is harnessed to peaceful projects I imagine it will make a big change in the living standards of the world.

I only have a few more minutes till morning colors and then it's "all hands turn to"! So I'll say so long for now.

Love to all,

James Behan T.M. 3/c

Jim

78

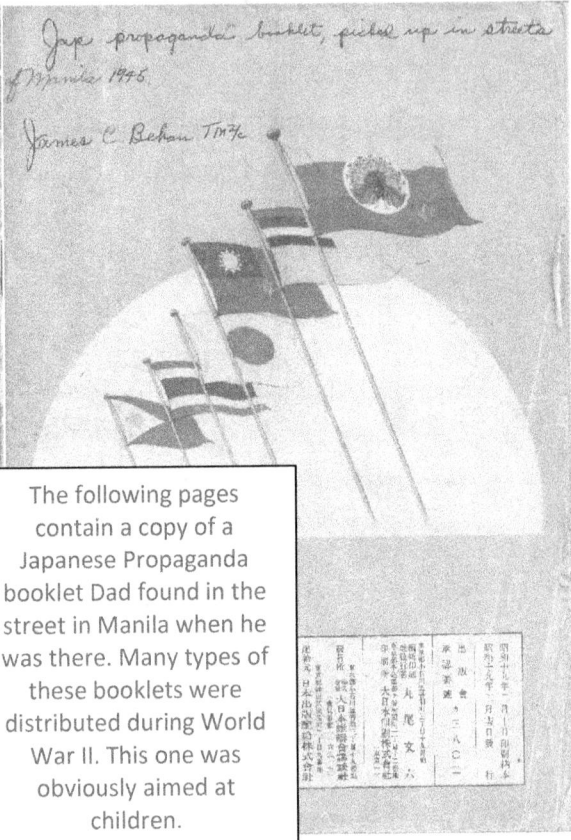

The following pages contain a copy of a Japanese Propaganda booklet Dad found in the street in Manila when he was there. Many types of these booklets were distributed during World War II. This one was obviously aimed at children.

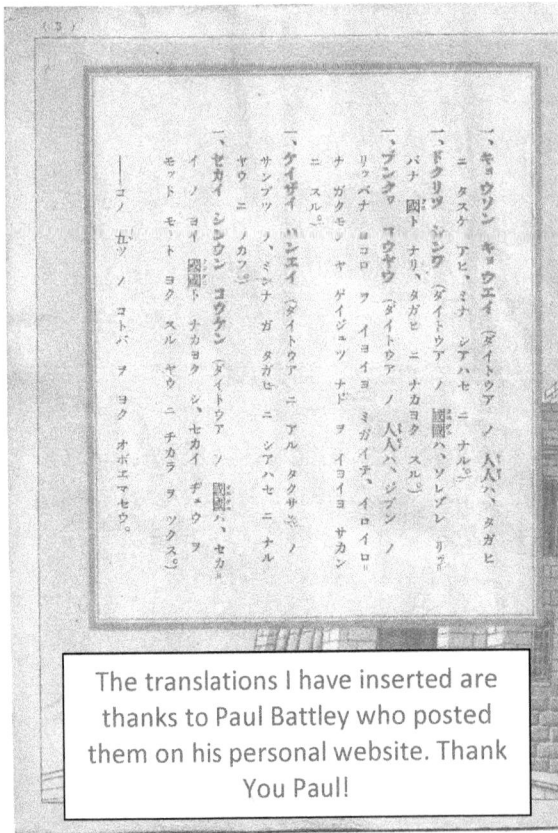

The translations I have inserted are thanks to Paul Battley who posted them on his personal website. Thank You Paul!

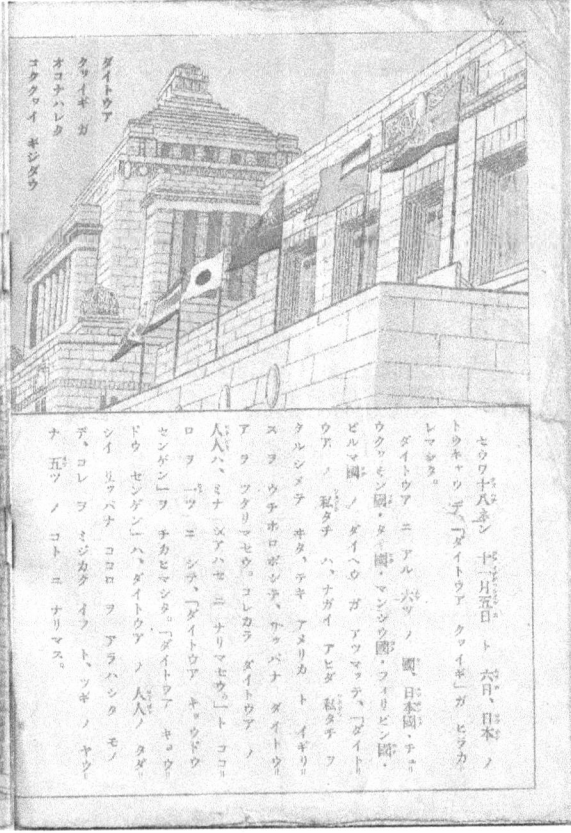

オゴソカナ ダイトウア クワイギ

「ダイトウア センゲン」ガ キマツタ トキ、ベツ ノ エノ ダイヘウ ハ、ミナ タチ アガツテ サンセイ ナサイ マシタ。

コノ エノ マンニ、中ニ オ立チ ニ ナツ テキルノ ハ、日本 國ノ ソウリダイジン 東條英機 カクカ デス。ソノ ヒダリ ガ チユーワミン國 ノ 汪情衞 カクカ ノ

ソノ ツギ ガ マンシウ國ノ 張景惠 カクカ、ビルマ國 カクカ デス。

カノ ミギ ハ、タイ國 ノ ワンワイタヤコン デンカ、フィリピン國 ノ ラウレル カクカ、ソノ ミギ ハ、ト゛クベツ ノ カンケイ デ、ジユウ インド ノ スバス・チヤンドラ・ボース カクカ デス。

ダイトウア ヲ クルシメル アクマ

アメリカ ヤ イギリス ヤ オランダ ハ、ジブン ノ タテ ノ タメ ナラ ドンナニ ワルイ コト デモ シマス。

(1) 四百ネン ホド マエ、ハジメテ ダイトウア ニ 來タ ヨーロツパ ジン ハ、ダイトウア ガ ユタカ デ、ホシイ モノ ガ アル ノデ、タカラ ニ、甘ツタ ラシク マシタ。

(2) オランダ ジン ハ、ジブンタチ ノ バカリ モウケル タメ、ジヤワ ノ 人人 ヲ、カンガヘ テ、ヒドイ メ ニ アハセマシタ。

ダイトウア ノ 人人 ヲ、ウシ ヤ ウマ ノ ヤウニ コキツカヒ、ソノ スキ ニ、アラソ ヒ ヲ サセテ、タガヒ ニ アラソ フ 國 ヲ ウバヒマシタ。

(3) アヘン ヲ ウリツケタ モ、イギリス ジン デス。アヘン ハ、イヅ ノ マニカ 人人 ヲ ヨワ ラセ、オソロシイ ドク デス。

イヘ ヲ ヤキ、タクサン ノ 人人 ヲ コロシマシタ。イギリス ハ インド ヤ ビルマ ヲ ウバヒマシタ。オランダ ハ ジヤワ、スマトラ、ボルネオ ナド ヲ ウバヒマシタ。アメリカ ハ フィリピン ノ モノ ニ シマシタ。インドシナ ヲ ジブン ノ モノ ニ シタ。

(4) イギリス ジン ハ、ヲツミ ノ ナイ、ビルマ ノ 人人 ヲ タクサン コロシ、國 ヲ ウバツテ シマヒマシタ。

四百ネン ノ アヒダ、ダイトウア ハ アクマ ノ タメ ニ クルシミ ツヅケマシタ。

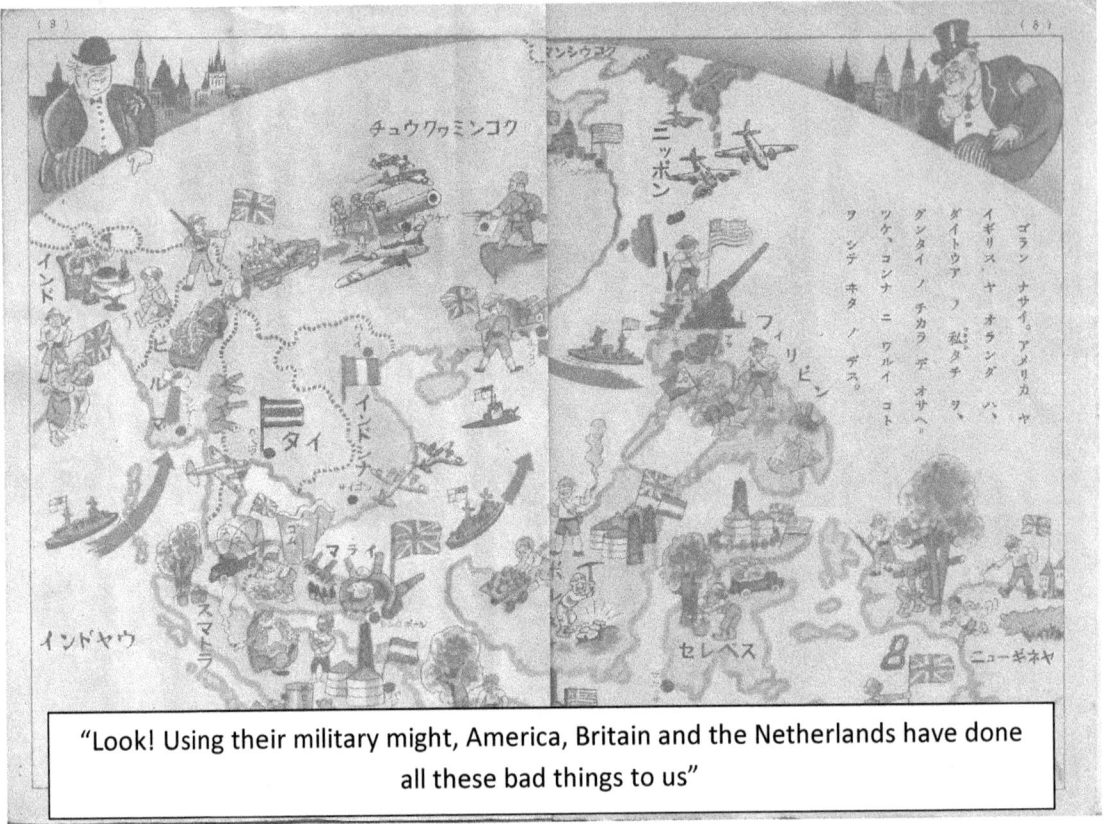
"Look! Using their military might, America, Britain and the Netherlands have done all these bad things to us"

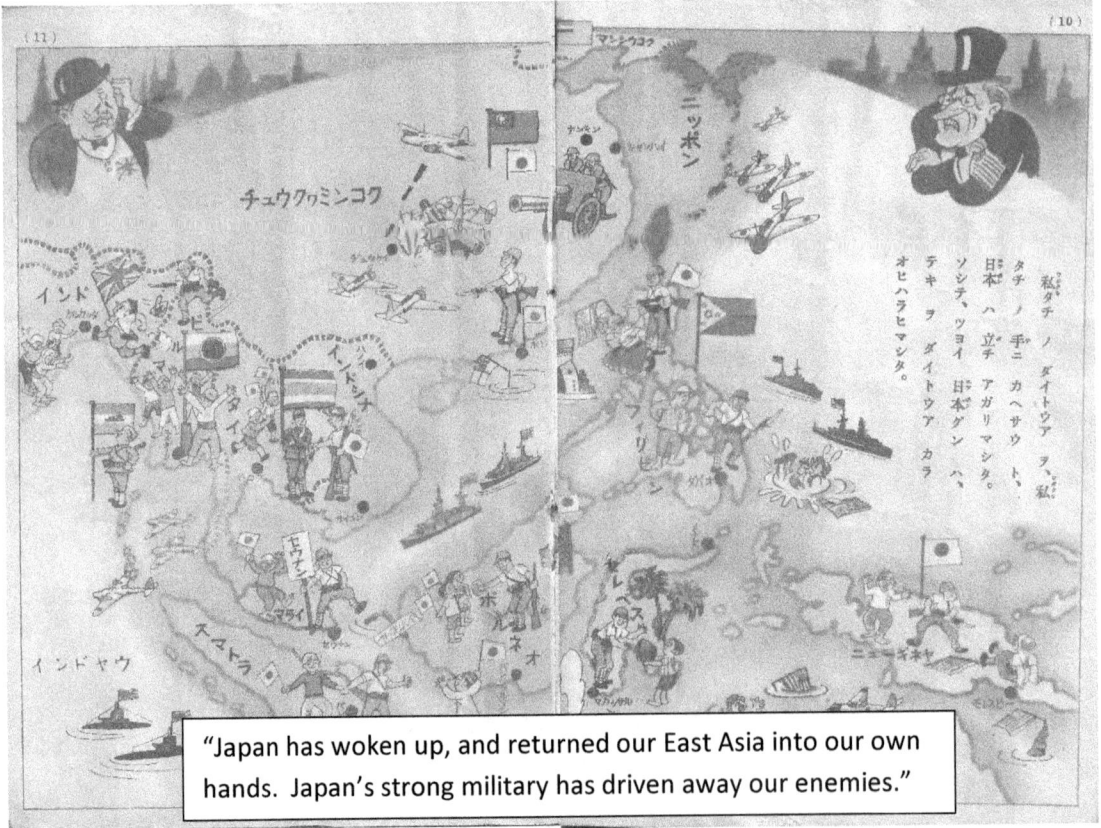
"Japan has woken up, and returned our East Asia into our own hands. Japan's strong military has driven away our enemies."

America, Britain, and the Netherlands were scared of East Asian prosperity; we must not forget this undeniable fact. If we have good relations and help each other, we shall definitely be happy.

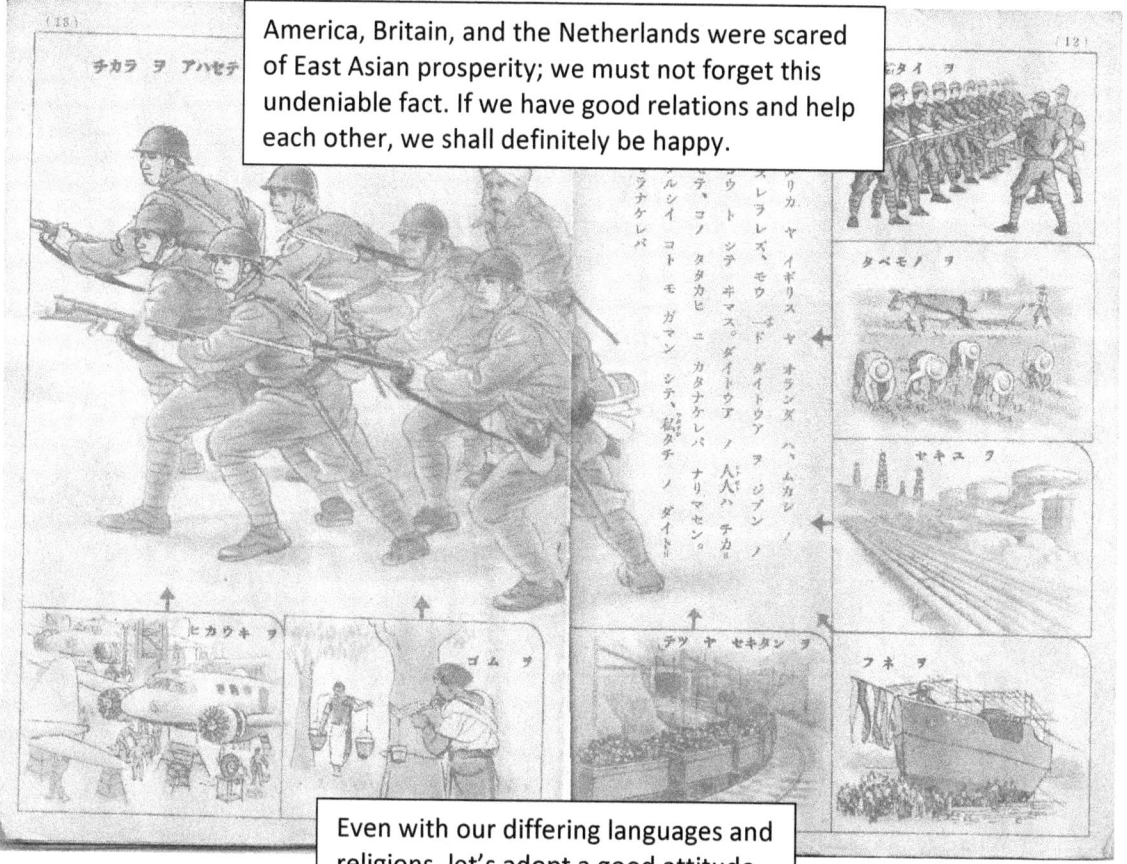

Even with our differing languages and religions, let's adopt a good attitude and be friendly like brothers. In happy times and sad, let's be friends.

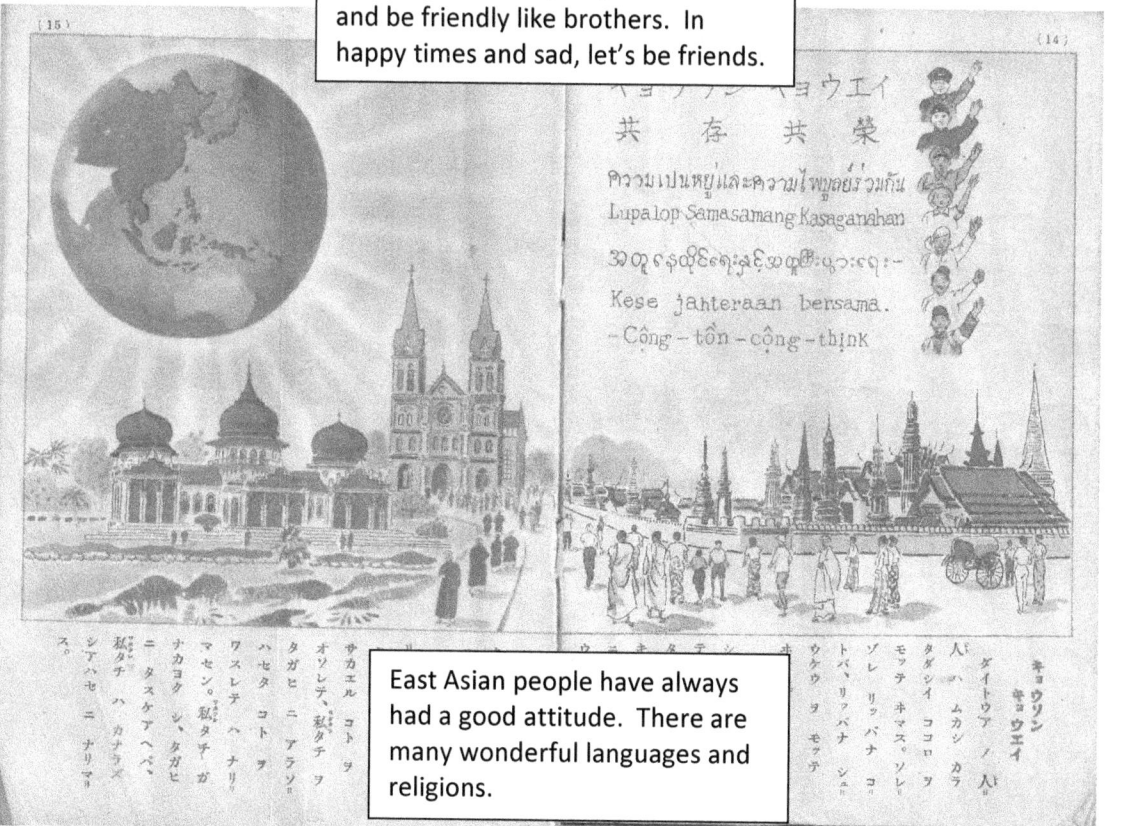

East Asian people have always had a good attitude. There are many wonderful languages and religions.

(16)

日本ト ドウメイ ヲ ムスンダ チュウクミン國

ツヨイ 日本

ドクリツ シタ フィリピン國

サカエ ユク マンシウ國

ドクリツ シ
ンワ

ウ國、
イマ、マンシ
デハ、ミナ
チカラ
ヲ アハセテ
ハタライテ キ
マス。
日本國ト チュ
ウクミン國ト
ハ、ドウメイ
ヲ ムスビマシ
タ。フィリピン
國ト ビルマ國
ハ、ドクリツ
シマシタ。タイ
國ハ 國ガ
ヒロク
ナリ

(17)

シアハセニ ナッタ ジャワ ヤ マライノ 人人

國ガ ヒロク ナッタ タイ國

イギリスヲ オヒハラウト シテ ヰル インドジン

ドクリツ シタ ビルマ國

マシタ。ジャワ
ヤ マライノ
人人モ、タイ
ツナ ヤクメ
ニ、ハタライテ
キマス。インド
ノ 人人ハ、
イギリス ヲ
オヒハラフト
シテ ヰマス。
イギリスノ
ダイトウアノ
國國ハ、ソレゾ
レリッパナ
國ニ ナリ、
タガヒニ
ナカヨク スル
ノデス。

(18)

日本ゴ ヲ ベンキャウ スル

日本語學校

ブンクヮ コウヤウ
アメリカ ヤ イギリス ヤ
オランダ ハ、私タチ ガ ドレ
ナ ベンキャウ シテ モ、

(19)

日本ニ 行ッテ ベンキャウ スル

ハタライテ モ、シアハセニ
シア クレマセン デシタ。シカ
シ、コレカラ ハ、ハタラケバ
ハタラク ホド、ベンキャウ
スレバ スル ホド、シアハセ
ニ ナリマス。
ヨク ベンキャウ シマセウ。
ソシテ、ダイトウアノ ブンク
ワ ヲ イヨイヨ サカン
ニ シマセウ。マタ ダイトウアノ
人人ガ タガヒニ ハナシ
アフ コトノ デキル ヤウ
ニ、日本ゴ ヲ マナビマセウ。

Pages 16 & 17 (On Top):

"Right now, in Manchuria, all the people are combining their strength and working together.

Japan and the Republic of China have formed an alliance. The Philippines and Burma have attained independence. Thailand has grown larger. The Javanese and Malays, too, are working on important business. India is driving away the British.

Next, the countries of East Asia will form a union and become a great power, friendly to one another."

Captions

The image captions are listed top-to-bottom, right-to-left:

7 5 3 1
8 6 4 2

1. A strong Japan.

2. A flourishing Manchuria.

3. A Republic of China in alliance with Japan.

4. An independent Philippines.

5. An expanded Thailand.

6. An independent Burma.

7. Happy Javanese and Malays.

8. The Indian army, chasing away the British.

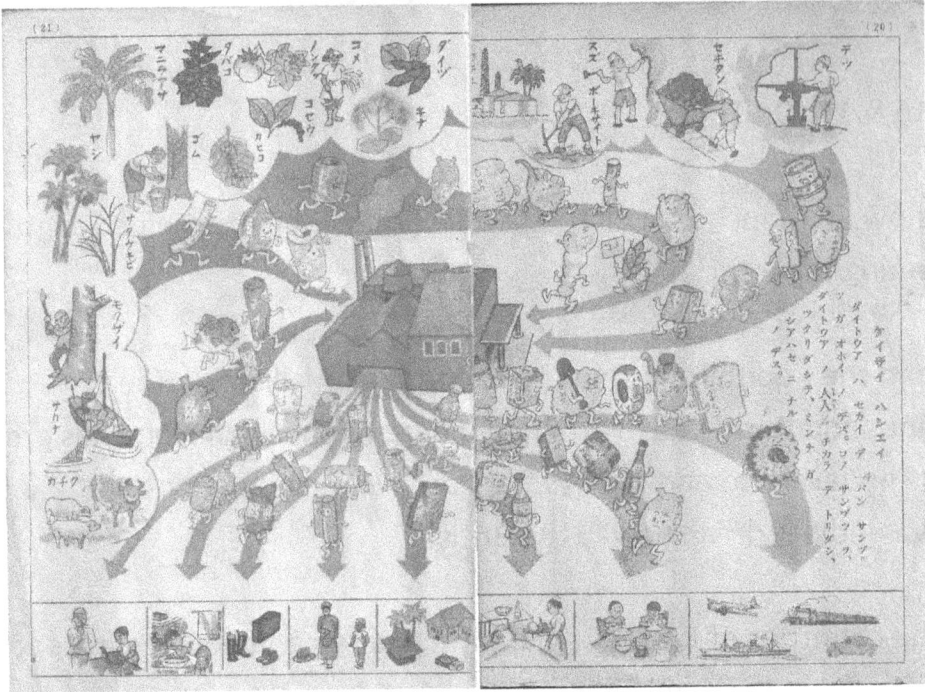

We people of East Asia have destroyed America and Britain with our combined strength. However, we are friendly with the good countries of the world. We study together and spread our superior culture over the world.

We will give other countries the products they need. We will make the world a much, much better place. We are of one heart. Let's walk together into the future, with our footsteps ringing out.

August 15th 1945
Victory Day

Dear Rose and All

The word has just been
passed over the P.A. "President Truman
has just announced that Japan has
surrendered and that the War is over.

Yippie !!!!

Love to All
Jim

James Behan T.M. 3/c

August 15th 1945
Victory Day

Dear Rose and all,

    The word has just been passed over the P.A. President Truman has just announced that Japan has surrendered and that the War is over.

Yippee!!!!!

Love to all

Jim

James Behan T.M. 3/c

Jap surrender party arrives

Manila City Hall

Although these pictures aren't labeled, I believe the one on the top right is from when General Douglas MacArthur spoke from Manila City hall to the Allied troops. The other pictures, as far as we can tell, are of the General and other U.S. Military leaders walking with the very unhappy-looking Japanese Commander.

• Surrender Or Die •

(Copy of a Leaflet Dropped on Corregidor Before Surrender)

TO HIS EXCELLENCY THE MAJOR-GENERAL JONATHAN WAINWRIGHT COMMANDER IN CHIEF OF THE UNITED STATES FORCES IN THE PHILIPPINES.

YOUR EXCELLENCY:

We have the honor to address you in accordance with the humanitarian principles of "BUSHIDO," the code of the Japanese warrior.

It will be recalled that some time ago, a note advising honorable surrender was sent to the Commander in Chief of your fighting forces. To this, as yet, no reply has been received.

Since our arrival in the Philippines with the Imperial Japanese Expeditionary Forces, already three months have elapsed, during which, despite the defeat of your allies, Britain and the Netherlands East Indies, and in the face of innumerable difficulties, the American and Filipino forces under your command have fought with much gallantry.

We are, however, now in a position to state that with men and supplies which surpass, both numerically and qualitatively, those under your command, we are entirely free, either to attack and put to rout your forces or to wait for the inevitable starvation of your troops within the narrow confines of the Bataan Peninsula.

Your excellency must be well aware of the future prospects of the Filipino-American forces under your command. To waste the valuable lives of these men in an utterly meaningless and hopeless struggle would be directly opposed to the principles of humanity, and, furthermore, such a course would sully the honor of a fighting man.

Your Excellency, you have already fought to the best of your ability. What dishonor is there in avoiding needless bloodshed? What disgrace is there following the defenders of Hong Kong, Singapore, and the Netherlands East Indies in the acceptance of honorable defeat? Your Excellency, your duty has been performed. Accept our sincere advice and save the lives of those officers and men under your command. The International Law will be strictly adhered to by the Imperial Japanese Forces and Your Excellency, those under your command will be saved and the delight and relief of their dear ones and families would be beyond the expression of words. We call upon you to reconsider this proposition with due thought.

If a reply to this advisory note is not received from your Excellency through special messenger by noon March 22nd, 1942, we shall consider ourselves at liberty to take any action whatsoever.

COMMANDER IN CHIEF OF
THE IMPERIAL JAPANESE ARMY & NAVY

(The following directive was printed on the reverse side of letter)
"ANYONE WHO GETS THIS LETTER IS REQUESTED TO SEND IT TO THE COMMANDER-IN-CHIEF OF THE UNITED STATES FORCES IN THE PHILIPPINES."

(This same directive was painted in black 5/16" letters on a red 1¾" cloth streamer two feet long. Streamer was attached to an empty beer can. White label on can bore the address and directive as above.)

Much to the amusement of the Allied Forces stationed on the Island of Corregidor, these leaflets were dropped there under cover of nightfall on January 29, 1942 by the Japanese. This island was where General MacArthur was stationed. The Japanese attempted to overtake Corregidor as part of their plan to eventually overtake Australia. Their loss during this battle, which lasted from December 29, 1941 through April of 1942, put a huge crimp in that plan. Many deaths and injuries were sustained by both sides.

| Extra | # Dobbin Press News | Extra |

U.S.S. DOBBIN (AD-8) — SUBIC BAY, P.I., WEDNESDAY, AUGUST 15, 1945

NIPPONESE SURRENDER

** ** **

WASHINGTON, D. C. Tuesday, August 14 (Special)—President Truman made the announcement at 8 a.m. Manila time, (that is 7 p.m. Tuesday, August 14th, Washington time), the Emperor of Japan stated his acceptance of Unconditional Surrender and ordered all Japanese Armed forces to cease operations and surrender their arms. President Truman has also ordered all United States Armed forces to suspend military operations. The President has also named General of the Army Douglas MacArthur as Allied Supreme Commander of Japan.

The announcement of the Japanese acceptance of Allied Unconditional Surrender was announced simultaneously in Washington, London, Moscow and Chunking. The Japanese note to the Allied Powers stated the acceptance of first the Potsdam declaration and the Allied note of August 11th which defined the powers of the Allied Supreme Commander over the Emperor. Hirohito's note also said that he was prepared to issue any orders that may be required by the Supreme Commander. Japanese Imperial headquarters has been ordered by the Emperor to effectuate the surrender by all Japanese Armed Forces. Although the Japanese have accepted surrender and both sides have ordered the cessation of military operations, it will not be V-J DAY officially until the formal signing of the surrender document takes place.

Following is the text of Japanese reply to the Allied counter proposal

"with reference to the announcement of August 10th, regarding the acceptance of the provisions of the Potsdam Declaration and the reply of the Government of the United States, Great Britain, Soviet Union and China, sent by Secretary of State Byrnes on August 11th, the Japanese Government has the honor to reply to the Government of the Four Powers as follows:

1.—His Majesty the Emperor has issued an Imperial Receipt regarding Japanese acceptance of the provisions of the Potsdam declaration.

2.—The Emperor is prepared to authorize and insure by and to his Government and the Imperial headquarters the necessary terms for carrying out the provisions of the Potsdam Declaration.

3.—His Majesty is also prepared to issue this communication to all military, naval and air authorities to issue to all forces under their control wherever located to cease active resistance and to surrender their arms."

For hours the official announcement of the surrender of the Slant-Eyed Rats had been expected, and officers and men were gathered around the various radio receivers aboard ship when the world-awaited announcement finally came through. There was considerable cheering, but no celebration. The crew of the Dobbin may not take part in the "Invasion-Occupation Ceremonies" in the Nips' liceland, but they are resolved to do THE job good and plenty when they invade the hotspots of a real live American city. But even though actual hostilities have ended, there will be an awful lot of supervising and policing of the rats, and probably some tough guerilla fighting. "Peace! Ain't it wonderful?"

MORE TAXES!

UNRRA Director General Lehman in a radio broadcast to the United States Saturday requested an additional $500,000,000 to meet increased relief requirements as a result of Far East developments and that Soviet requests for $700,000,000 in relief. Mr.

HARD WORKING CONGRESSMEN TO RETURN TO WORK

Senator Barkeley, upon leaving the White House Saturday after a ninety minute appointment with the President, announced that at the request of President Truman, Congress would be called back September 4th, about a month earlier than the scheduled October 8th, end of recess. Senator Barkeley listed the following five measures: 1. Amendment to the Social Security Laws. 2. Revision of the surplus property disposal act to provide, among the other things, for a single direction. 3. The full employment bill. 4. Continuation of such war agencies and powers as may be deemed essential for the reconversion period. 5. A bill to give the President sweeping powers to re-organize the executive branch of the Government. In preparation for the reconvening, committees will work to make emergency legislation ready for floor action.

Lehman explained that the amount of money needed for the coming year would exceed $2,000,000,000,000 instead of the original estimate of $1,500,000,000, he revealed that UNRRA has a program for sending 800,000 tons of relief supplies to China as soon as the Country's ports were open and the shipping situation permitted. The supplies have an estimated value of $192,000,000 and are made up mostly of agricultural machinery, earth moving equipment and productive machinery.

Trial of Hun War Criminals

Trials of major war criminals at Nurenberg for which preparations are being made according to completed war agreement will mark the milestone in progress toward world security, Senator Alexander Wiley of Wisconsin said today. Wiley is ranking minority member of United States Senate Judiciary committee and member of Foreign Relations committee Wiley said only as we fix and exact penalties upon war criminals can we hope to control such excesses. It is a long step forward to our goal of World Security that making war now has been made a punishable crime. It is one of the great achievements of our time that four powers have arrived at complete unity and

agreement on this principle and have incorporated it in their International Military Tribunal. Even as a way for swift and just trials of some 52 major war criminals is cleared comes statistical evidence of thoroughness with which Nazis exterminated Jews, political opponents and deported to Germany. Of some four hundred thousand persons all deported to Germany from France, Belgium, Holland and Norway during occupation, less than 50,000 have been found and repatriated leaving a toll of dead and missing at 350,000 for these countries alone. Jews deported to Germany from these same countries totaled 234,000 and total repatriated up to July 20th less than 10,000. These figures are clear evidence of Nazi systematic large scale extermination of whole groups and classes of people.

19, September, 1945

Dear Rose and all;

Received the two boxes of photographic material yesterday. That printing frame is just what I wanted. I was surprised to find the two rolls of film with the cookies. Everything is swell Rose, I appreciate all the trouble you went to to get these things. The cookies were fresh, and unbroken, and delicious! I guess I'll have plenty of gum chewing to do for a while. Thanks a lot for everything.

I have no news of any importance. Everything is the same. Still a lot of stateside talk going on, but it's a lot of baloney. I'll believe it when the old man orders the going home pennant broke out, but not until. A year ago they were saying the same thing so I haven't much faith in anything anymore.

I received a letter from cookie's mother thanking me for sending her a card. She said everyone in Brantford was okay and that the boys were hoping for a discharge from the army.

VJ Day Fireworks

7th Fleet Recreation – Subic Bay 1945

I am enclosing a few small prints I ran off yesterday. I thought you might enjoy them or here they are.

How is everyone at home? I suppose the old routine has settled in again now that school has started. Maybe in a few more months, I'll have another sentence at the breakfast table. Sure will be good to sit down and act like a human being again.

Say hello and give everyone my regards. So long for a little while.

Love,
Jim

P.S. Thanks again for everything !!

19, September, 1945

Dear Rose & All,

Received the two boxes of photographic material yesterday. That printing frame is just what I wanted. I was surprised to find the two rolls of film with the cookies. Everything is swell Rose, I appreciate all the trouble you went to, to get these things. The cookies were fresh and unbroken, and delicious. I guess I'll have plenty of gum chewing to do for a while. Thanks a lot for everything.

I received a letter from Cookie's mother thanking me for sending her a card. She said everyone in Brantford was okay and that the boys were hoping for a discharge from the Army.

I am enclosing a few small prints I ran off yesterday. Thought you might enjoy them so here they are.

How is everyone at home? I suppose the old routine has settled in again now that school has started. Maybe in a few more months you'll have another customer at the breakfast table. Sure will be good to sit down and eat like a human being again.

Say hello and give everyone my regards. So long for a little while.

Love,

Jim

P.S. Thanks again for everything!!

Nov. 2, 1945
Subic Bay

Dear Rose & all

Put another plate on the table
I'm coming home. We are leaving for
Samar today to go in dry dock. We will
leave Samar Nov 15th for San Francisco.
If all goes well and I get first
section leave I ought to make it by
Christmas. Don't write or send any more
packages. I will write you or call
as soon as we hit Frisco.

The Skipper just announced this
good news over the ball horn. The crew
is going wild, everyone is yelling to beat
hell and dancing all over the place.

Yesterday I made T.M. 3/c. which means
another stripe and a few more bucks

each month. I'm so darn nervous I
can hardly hold this pen. I have been assigned
a wheel watch for the trip. Brother I don't
need a compass, I can smell the states
already. We have about 7000 miles to go
and we may stop at Pearl Harbor. If
we do I will write you from there. Even
if I don't make it in time for Christmas
I think this will be the happiest
Christmas we had in a long time.
                    Be Seeing You

                    Love to All
                    Jim

P.S.
I will buy a coat in Frisco so
don't worry about me catching cold.

Nov. 2, 1945
Subic Bay

Dear Rose & All,

Put another plate on the table I'm coming home. We are leaving for Samar today to go in dry dock. We will leave Samar Nov. 15th for San Francisco. If all goes well and I get first section leave I ought to make it by Christmas. Don't write or send any more packages. I will write you or call as soon as we hit Frisco.

The Skipper just announced this good news over the bull horn. The crew is going wild, everyone is yelling to beat hell and dancing all over the place.

Yesterday I made T.M. 2/c. Which means another stripe and a few more bucks each month. I'm so darn nervous I can hardly hold this pen. I have been assigned as wheel watch for the trip. Brother I don't need a compass, I can smell the states already. We have about 7000 miles to go and we may stop at Pearl Harbor. If we do I will write you from there. Even if I don't make it in time for Christmas I think this will be the happiest Christmas I've had in a long time.

Be Seeing you
Love to All,
Jim

P.S. I will buy a coat in Frisco so
don't worry about me catching cold.

December 8, 1945
San Diego Bay

Dear Rose and all,

We arrived in the states yesterday afternoon about 3:00 o'clock. So far I haven't been able to get ashore, so am having one of my buddies send you a telegram this afternoon. The 30 day leave parties are being made up now. Half the crew will go first and the other half as soon as the first group returns. I don't know which group I'll be in but anyway I'm pretty sure of coming home now or some time in January. When we were about half way across our orders were changed from Frisco to Dago. It surprised us but anyway it's wonderful to see the states.

Welcome Home – San Diego
1945

San Diego Harbor
Water Taxi

Last night I had a glass of ice cold milk, I could have drank a gallon but they only gave us one glass look. As soon as I get my first liberty I will. I have no idea when it will be but don't be surprised if we wake you up in the middle of the night. We had a rough trip most of the way so we lost about two days time. Don't send any of my clothes until I write for them. I will pick up another coat here if I make the first leave party. This is all I have to say now. Say hello to everyone. So Long.

Love to all
Jim

95

December 8, 1945
San Diego Bay

Dear Rose & All,

We arrived in the states yesterday afternoon about 3:00 O'clock. So far I haven't been able to get ashore. I am having one of my buddies send you a telegram this afternoon. The 30 day leave parties are being made up now. Half the crew will go first and the other half as soon as the first group returns. I don't know which group I'll be in but anyway I'm pretty sure of coming home now or sometime in January. When we were about half way across our orders were changed from Frisco to Dago. It surprised us but anyway it's wonderful to see the states.

Last night I had a glass of ice cold milk, I could have drank a gallon but they only gave us one glass each.

As soon as I get my first liberty I'll call. I have no idea when it will be but don't be surprised if I wake you up in the middle of the night.

We had a rough trip most of the way so we lost about two days' time. Don't send any of my clothes until I write for them. I will pick up another coat if I make the first leave party. This is all I have to say now. Say hello to everyone. So Long.

Love to All,

Jim

MARCH 2 1946

Dear Rose and All,

"Thirty days" said the Judge!!!
That's all that stands between me and my
"ruptured duck" My buddie Joe is leaving for
home tomorrow for his discharge. Bradley
leaves the 15th and I'm taking up the tail
on April 2nd. The crap is getting deeper and
harder to take each day. All the little "Gods"
are thundering with authority. Boy what a
sweet day April 2nd will be.

I'm sorry your having so much
cold weather. It's very nice here now, but
I'll take the snow. There really isn't any
news of importance to tell. The strike
is getting more disgusting every time I
hear the news. If the Russians are going
to start another war I hope they wait till
I get out.

I'll close for now. Say hello to
everyone for me.

Love to All
Jim

Behan - San Diego - 1946

Souvenir from

THE VILLA
Downstairs in the Wm. Penn Hotel

RESTAURANT

Your Hosts
LOU ⟷ FREDDY

OPEN
EVERY DAY
5 PM-2 AM

509 F Street
SAN DIEGO
CALIF.

FOR
RESERVATIONS

FINE ITALIAN FOODS
IMPORTED AND DOMESTIC
BEERS and WINES

call
F·0764

March 2, 1946

Dear Rose & All,

"Thirty days" said the Judge!!!

That's all that stands between me and my "ruptured duck". My buddie Joe is leaving for home tomorrow for his discharge. Bradley leaves the 15th and I'm taking up the tail on April 2nd. The crap is getting deeper and harder to take each day. All the little "Gods" are thundering with authority. Boy what a sweet day April 2nd will be.

I'm sorry you're having so much cold weather. It's very nice here now, but I'll take the snow. There really isn't any news of importance to tell. The strike is getting more disgusting every time I hear the news. If the Russians start another war I hope they wait till I get out.

I'll close for now. Say hello to everyone for me.

Love to All,

Jim.

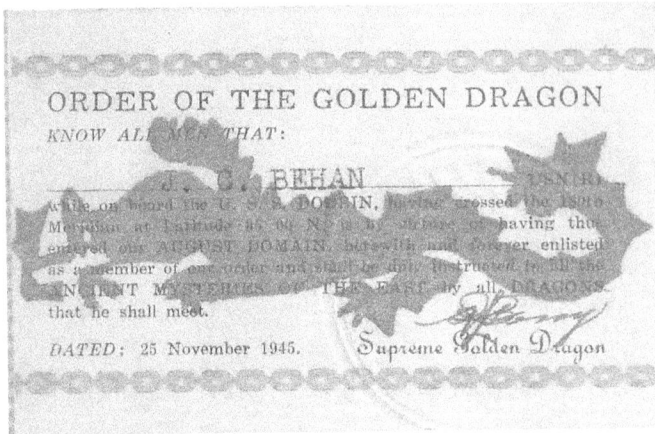

Membership Card for having
crossed the International Dateline

ORDER OF THE GOLDEN DRAGON

KNOW ALL MEN THAT:

___J. C. BEHAN___   USN (R)

While on board the U. S. S. DOBBIN, having crossed the 180th Meridian at Latitude 35 00 N, is by virtue of having thus entered our AUGUST DOMAIN, herewith and forever enlisted as a member of our order and shall be duly instructed in all the ANCIENT MYSTERIES OF THE EAST by all DRAGONS that he shall meet.

DATED: 25 November 1945   Supreme Golden Dragon

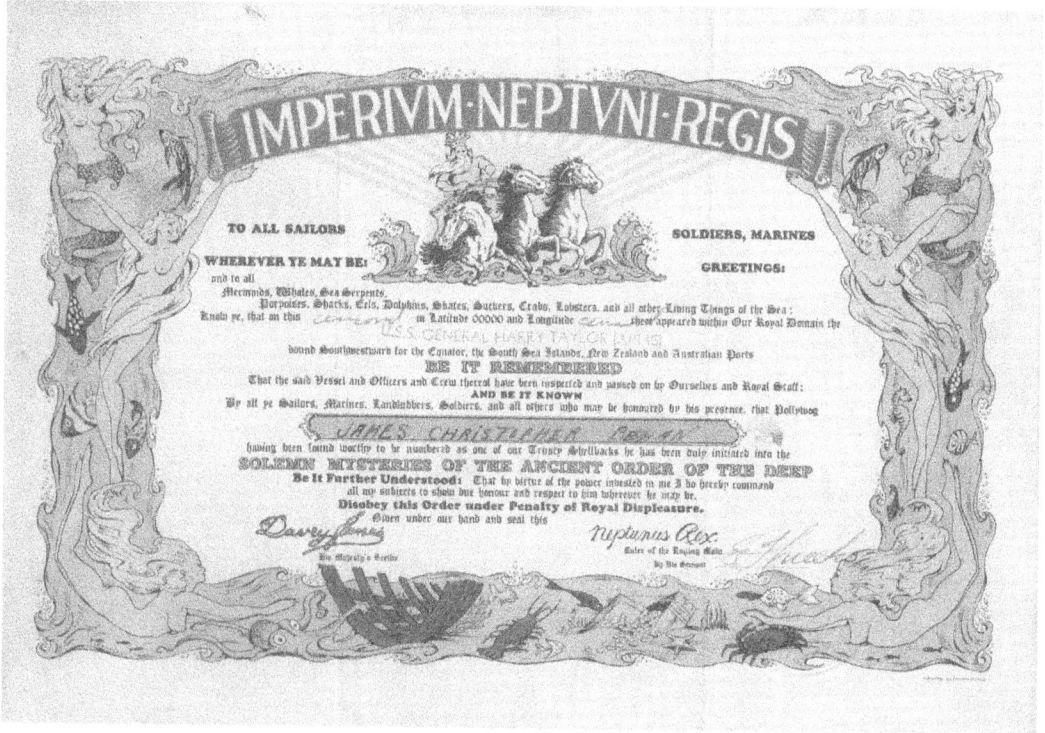

Certificate for having sailed across the equator for the first time
– graduating from being a "Pollywog" to a "Shellback" and having
passed a series of tests and trials by King Neptune.

Note the latitude & longitude numbers have been censored out.

Jim Behan - WW II

June 6, 1943 - Graduated from St. Michael's High School, Flint, Mich

July - 1943 - Enlisted in U.S. Navy & Sent to Great Lakes Boot Camp

July - 1943 - Assigned to Co. #1318

August - 1943 - Graduated from Boot Camp as Apprentic Seasman

Sept. - 1943 - Sent to Fleet Torpedo School, Norfolk, Va.

Dec. - 1943 - Graduated from FTS as S 1/c (Seaman 1rst Class)

Christmas - 1943 - 10 Days Leave for Christmas

Jan. - 1944 - Shipped to Advance Torpedo School in San Diego, Cal.

May - 1944 - Graduated from Advance Torp. School as Torpedoman 3/c

May - 1944 - Shipped to San Francisco to be Shipped Overseas
   After having Trained aboard U.S.S. Robinson (D.D. 562) in Firing
   Torpedos and Depth Charges)

June 1944 - Put on Temprary Shore Patrol while waiting for a Troop Shi

June 1944 - Boarded "U.S.S. General Harry Taylor (its maiden voyage). Passed
   Alcatraz and the Golden Gate and wondered if we would
   ever see again. Passed Hawaii headed SW. after 5 days

July 1944 - After 21 Days at a Harbor called "Milne Bay, New Guinea.
   After 28 Days we (Boarde) U.S.S. Ward which had fired the
   first shot at Pearl Harbor

July 1944 - Three weeks Traveling N.E. along the New Guinea cost, the
   Ward Skipper fired at Jap emplacements along the way.

July 1944 - We arrived at Hollandias Humbolt Bay in Dutch New Guinea.

July 1944 - We left the "Ward" and went ashore and pitched our
   tents on the beach at the Jungles Edge. After Three
   Days and nights with Armed Sentries (Japs still active in the
   neighborhood) we Boarded the Dobbin (AD3) which had Just
   Arrived. (What a Relief)

August - 94 - Dobbin Hauls Anchor and we head for the Phillipines
   We are 24 Hr Combat watch because of the Jap
   Kamikazes. We hear that the U.S.S. Ward had Been

SUNK BY THE JAPS KAMIKAZIES, WITH VERY FEW SURVIVORS.
WHEN WE REACH THE PHILLIPINES WE WERE SENT TO SUBIC BAY.
(MANILA BAY WAS STILL UNDER FIRE).

OUR CAPT. HAD ARMED SENTRIES POSTED - BOW, STERN & AMIDSHIP.
THE JAPS WOULD TRY TO SWIM OUT FROM THE BEACH AND BLOW US UP,
ESPECIALLY AT NIGHT. OUR JOB WAS TO PROVIDE TORPEDOS AMMO, FOOD AND MEDICAL
SUPPORT FOR OUR SQUADRON OF DESTROYERS.

AFTER THE TWO ATOMIC BOMBS WERE DROPPED THE JAPS SENT
THEIR NEGOTIATORS BY PLANE TO MANILA. WE WERE TOLD NOT TO
FIRE ON THEM (THEY WERE PAINTED) WITH "GREEN CROSSES" ON THE
SIDES OF THE AIRCRAFT THAT TRANSPORTED THEM TO MANILA
FROM JAPAN.

A WEEK LATER THEY FLEW OVER US. THE NEXT DAY OUR SKIPPER
GAVE ONE HALF THE CREW A WEEKEND PASS TO MANILA. WE
WENT DOWN TO MANILA BAY ON AN AUSTRALIAN HEAVY CRUISER
THAT WAS GOING THAT WAY. WE HAD OUR EYES FULL BECAUSE
MANILA WAS IN TERRIBLE SHAPE AND THE PEOPLE WERE STARVING
WE BROUGHT FOOD WITH US FOR THEM. WE GOT OUR EYES
FULL ON THE ~~DEATH~~ DISTRUCTION AND SUFFERING. WE LEFT FOR
SAN DIEGO IN SIX WEEKS.
GOT AN "HONORABLE DISCHARGE" IN APRIL 1946

DAD

Jim Behan - WWII

June 6, 1943 – Graduated from St. Michael's High School, Flint, Mich

July, 1943 – Enlisted in US Navy & sent to Great Lakes Boot Camp

July, 1943 – Assigned to Co. #1318

August, 1943 – Graduated from boot camp as apprentice Seaman

Sept., 1943 – Sent to Fleet Torpedo School, Norfolk, VA

Dec., 1943 – Graduated from FTS as S 1/c (Seaman 1st Class)

Christmas, 1943 – 10 days leave for Christmas

Jan., 1944 – Shipped to Advance Torpedo School in San Diego, Cal.

May, 1944 – Graduated from Advance Torpedo School as Torpedo Man 3/c

May, 1944 – Shipped to San Francisco to be shipped overseas after having trained aboard USS Robinson (D.D. 562 in Firing Torpedos and Depth Charges)

June, 1944 – Put on temporary shore patrol while waiting for a troop ship

June, 1944 - Boarded "U.S.S. General Harry Taylor" (it's maiden voyage). Passed Alcatraz and the Golden Gate and wondered if we would ever see them again. Passed Hawaii, headed S.W. after 5 days

July, 1944 – After 21 days arrived at a harbor called "Milne Bay" New Guinea. After 28 days we board U.S.S. Ward which had fired the first shot at earl Harbor, on a Jap midget sub.

July, 1944 – Three weeks travelling N.E. along the New Guinea coast, the Ward Skipper fired at Jap emplacements along the way.

July, 1944 – We arrived at Holland in Humbolt Bay in Dutch New Guinea

July, 1944 – We left the "Ward" and went ashore and pitched our tents on the beach at the Jungle's edge. After three days and nights with armed Sentries (Japs still active in the neighborhood) we boarded the Dobbin (AD3) which had just arrived (what a relief)

August, 1944 – Dobbin hauls anchor and we head for the Philippines. We have 24 Hr combat watch because of the Jap Kamikazes. We hear that The U.S.S. Ward had been sunk by the Jap Kamikazes, with very few survivors.

When we reach the Philippines we were sent to Subic Bay. (Manila was still under fire).

Our Capt. Had armed sentries posted – bow, stern & at midship. The Japs would try to swim out from the beach and blow us up, especially at night. Our job was to provide torpedoes, ammo, depth charges, food & medical support for our squadron of destroyers.

After the two atomic bombs were dropped the Japs sent their negotiators by plane to Manila. We were told not to fire on them (they were painted) with "green crosses" on the sides of the aircraft that transported them to Manila from Japan.

A week later they flew over us. The next day our Skipper gave one half the crew a weekend pass to Manila. We went down to Manila Bay on an Australian heavy cruiser that was going that way. We had our eyes full because Manila was in terrible shape and the people were starving. We brought food with us for them. We got our eyes full on the destruction and suffering. We left for San Diego in six weeks.

Got an "Honorable Discharge" in April 1946

Dad

Tom (T.C.) BRADLEY TM3/C
Jim BEHAN TM3/C
DOWN TOWN SAN DIEGO, CA. EARLY 1946 AWAITING DISCHARGE AFTER WAR'S END

Tom (T.C.) Bradley TM 3/c
Jim Behan TM 2/c
Downtown San Diego, CA. Early 1946
Awaiting discharge after war's end

Division of Naval History

Ships' Histories Section

Navy Department

HISTORY OF USS DOBBIN (AD 3)

One of the few ships which went through the entire war without returning once to the United States, USS DOBBIN contributed to the success of the Pacific campaign by serving as a hospital ship, station ship and supply ship in addition to her regular duties as a destroyer tender.

The tender, named in memory of the Honorable James Cochrane Dobbin, Secretary of the Navy from 1853 to 1857, was built in the Navy Yard, Philadelphia, Pennsylvania. Her keel was laid there on 23 December 1919 and she was launched on 5 May 1921. Mrs. Herbert H. James, a granddaughter of the ship's namesake, served as sponsor. USS DOBBIN was placed in commission on 23 July 1924.

USS DOBBIN was lying in Pearl Harbor with five of her charges alongside for tender overhaul on 7 December 1941, when the Japanese launched their surprise attack. Breaking out all her spare machine guns, the ship helped repel the planes with no loss, as repair crews worked feverishly to get machinery back together. Only three bombs came close to the tender, spraying the stern with fragments which injured several men.

The attack left plenty of work for DOBBIN to do, and, under the direction of her commanding officer Captain H.E. Paddock, USN, she immediately began repairing battle damage. She remained in the area until the Spring of 1942, when she was detached from Destroyers, Battle Force, and reported for duty with the SEVENTH Fleet in Sydney, Australia.

The ship stayed in Sydney for a year, furnishing services and overhaul to everything from patrol craft to cruisers. On 25 June 1943 she began a series of moves forward, proceeding to Milne Bay, New Guinea, via Brisbane, Mackay and Pownsville, Australia.

Late in January 1944, DOBBIN left New Guinea for Sydney, where she was to undergo an overhaul herself. By 27 February she was back on station, remaining in the New Guinea area until June 1944. On 26 May 1944 Captain S.Y. Cutler, USN, relieved Captain H.N. Williams, USN, as commanding officer.

As the battle lines moved westward across the Pacific, the tender moved along, always staying in the forward areas in order to be readily accessible for the damaged ships of the battle force. On 6 June 1944, she sailed for Manus Island, returning to the big staging areas at Medang and Hollandia, New Guinea, in July. In mid-February 1945, she joined a convoy for Subic Bay, Luzon, being one of the first ships of the service Force to arrive.

Captain Cutler was relieved as commanding officer by Captain J.T. Warren, USN, on 3 May 1945.

DOBBIN remained in the Philippines to offer services and repair through the rest of the war. On 14 November 1945, she got underway for San Diego, California, for her first sight of the United States since the war began.

By a Directive of December 1946, USS DOBBIN was stricken and disposed of through the War Shipping Administration.

USS DOBBIN earned one Battle Star on the Asiatic-Pacific Area Service Medal for the Pearl Harbor attack on 7 December 1941.

Destroyer
Pin

U S Navy
League Pin

U.S. Naval Reserve
Honorable Discharge Pin

Ruptured Duck Pin

American	Asiatic Pacific	Philippine Liberation

Campaign Ribbon

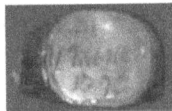

Manila
10-45 Ring

BACK OF
MEDAL

American
Campaign
Medal

Asiatic
Pacific
Campaign
Medal

Philippine
Liberation
Medal

World War II
Victory Medal

"Torpedo Man"
Uniform Patch

Dog Tag

Ruptured Duck
Uniform Patch

US Veterans
of Foreign
Wars Tie Pin

Epilogue

By reading this you have travelled along with what I would now consider a "child" fresh out of high school with fire in his eyes and patriotism in his soul heading off to fight in a war with no reservation, no question of "should I?" He was alongside thousands of other young people, many of whom did not return alive. They had the memories of the Great Depression still fresh in their minds and the anger in their hearts that comes from a military attack on their homeland.

I realize that this material will, of course, be of interest to those who were "there" during World War II – both at home and abroad. I also hope that those who are of a younger age, who may not have taken the time to really learn about WWII until now, will realize what it was like for those who served in the Military during **_all_** wars as well as those who waited and prayed for them to return home safely. I can say without hesitation that this has been the case for me. I never truly understood before.

I wish as well that anyone who reads this book will come to know that anyone who has had to leave their home during any war experiences _at least_ what my Dad experienced... and so much more.

It is not just because these letters were written by my Father that they drew me in and held my interest in wondering "what happens next". It's a true feeling of gratitude and pride as well as real amazement at the courage these so-very-young people had.

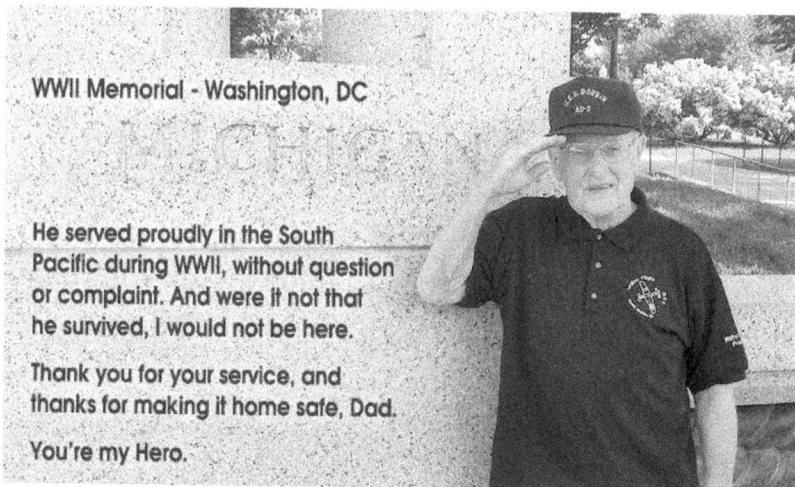

WWII Memorial - Washington, DC

He served proudly in the South Pacific during WWII, without question or complaint. And were it not that he survived, I would not be here.

Thank you for your service, and thanks for making it home safe, Dad.

You're my Hero.

About the Covers

The front cover is a recreation of a 1945 Sunday dinner table using authentic items. The dishes were my Father's Mother's china, and the crystal goblets were hers as well. The chairs are all antique; the one at the end in the foreground has a seat that was covered with hand-stitched needlepoint by my Mother's Mother. There is a genuine 1942 radio and 1901 Singer sewing machine in the background. Dad's Mother's portrait is on top of the sewing machine with a hand-made doily beneath it. The tablecloth belonged to my Mother and we had many holiday dinners on it. On the wall in the background is a portrait of my Father at the age of two in an antique frame. My vision is for you to "see" that someone is missing, that there's an empty chair, awaiting the return of its occupant.

The back cover is an artful compilation of 3 photos of my Father, put together by my brother, Dan Behan. The one on the left is his High School Senior picture. On the right is his boot camp picture. The middle one was taken by my brother Paul when he and Dad visited the World War II Memorial in Washington DC in 2011. The actual letters in this book are in the possession of yet another brother, Mike, who was kind enough to entrust them to me for this project. The photo albums are with my niece, Katie, who lives in Mississippi and was also kind enough to entrust them to me. My sister, Maryanne, worked tirelessly to take care of Dad's will and estate and did an excellent job. We all lost our brother, Tom, in 2009. He loved talking about the war with Dad. Mom left us in 2008 after a wonderful life with Dad. Thank you to my whole family for your contribution here – both literally and morally.

www.ingramcontent.com/pod-product-compliance
Lightning Source LLC
Chambersburg PA
CBHW081542040426

42448CB00015B/3194